Cai

ILLUSTRATED

written and photographed by

Michael Haag

THE AMERICAN UNIVERSITY IN CAIRO PRESS
CAIRO • NEW YORK

Contents

An Outline of People and Events including maps of the city   3

Old Cairo   8

The Coptic Museum   14

Fustat   17

The Mosque of Ibn Tulun and the Gayer-Anderson House   18

The Citadel   22

The Southern Quarters   28

The Sultan Hasan and Rifai Mosques   32

Al-Azhar Park   37

Darb al-Ahmar   38

The Islamic Museum   44

From Bab Zuwayla to al-Azhar   46

Khan al-Khalili   52

The Heart of Medieval Cairo   56

Bayt al-Suhaymi   62

The Mosque of al-Hakim and the Northern Gates   67

The City of the Dead   68

Downtown Cairo   72

Garden City   78

Manyal Palace   81

Gezira   82

The Egyptian Museum   88

Memphis and Saqqara   92

The Pyramids   94

Michael Haag is a London-based writer and photographer. He is the author of *Alexandria: City of Memory*, published by Yale University Press and The American University in Cairo Press, and *Alexandria Illustrated*, published by The American University in Cairo Press.

I dedicate this book to Zizi Niazi Badr and Mohamed Badr.

Front cover: The Badestan in Khan al-Khalili.
Back cover: The Pyramids at Giza.

Title page illustration: The Narmer Palette, which dates from around 3000 B.C., is one of the earliest examples of hieroglyphic writing. It reads: "The falcon god Horus leads captive the inhabitants of the papyrus country." The papyrus country is Lower Egypt. The falcon god Horus is Narmer himself, otherwise known as Menes, who came from Upper Egypt. As the first king of a united Egypt, he built his capital at Memphis. Present-day Cairo is the heir to ancient Memphis. The Narmer Palette is on view at the Egyptian Museum in Cairo.

Published in Egypt in 2006 by
The American University in Cairo Press
113 Sharia Kasr el Aini, Cairo, Egypt
420 Fifth Avenue, New York, NY 10018
www.aucpress.com

Photograph of Narmer Palette on page 1 by Araldo De Luca/Archivo White Star. Photographs on page 44 and 45 (top left and center left) by Boulos Isaac. Photograph on page 45 (top right) by Colin Elgie. All other photographs by Michael Haag.

Dar el Kutub no. 2838/05
ISBN 977 424 935 6

Layout by Mina Anis/AUC Press Design Center

Printed in Egypt

Above: Greater Cairo, with a population of eighteen million, is the largest city of Africa, of Islam, and of the countries round the Mediterranean. It spans both sides of the Nile, the longest river in the world.

The Nile is like a great lung that breathes life into the congested city, the most densely populated urban area on earth. The river flows northward through Cairo at five kilometers an hour, while a wind blows in from the Mediterranean nine days out of ten. Cairo is here because of the river, and the city has crept northward over the centuries—from Fustat of the Arab conquest, to al-Qatai of Ibn Tulun, to al-Qahira of the Fatimids, to modern-day Zamalek on the island of Gezira—to seek out the freshening breeze.

Here the view is toward central Cairo from the top of the Cairo Tower on Gezira; connecting both sides of the river, the Sixth of October Bridge is part of an interconnecting series of highways, flyovers, and bridges that took thirty years to build.

But as the sun sets over the Nile, the present slips away into timelessness. The call of the muezzins floating across the darkening city and the Pyramids of Giza, magnificently silhouetted against the shimmering horizon, are reminders that the monuments of pharaohs and sultans lie within the compass of the city Egyptians call 'Mother of the World.'

An Outline of People and Events

3000–332 B.C.: The Pharaonic Period

In about 3000 B.C. Egypt is united by King **Menes** (a.k.a. **Narmer**). He founds Memphis which, like present-day Cairo situated twenty kilometers to the north, commands both the Nile Valley and the Delta.

During the **Old Kingdom** (2686–2125 B.C.) the Step Pyramid is built by King **Zoser** (r. 2667–2648 B.C.) at Saqqara, and the first true pyramids are built at Giza by **Cheops** (r. 2589–2566 B.C.), **Chephren** (r. 2558–2532 B.C.) and **Mycerinus** (r. 2532–2503 B.C.).

331 B.C.–A.D. 642: The Greco-Roman and Christian Periods

In 331 B.C. **Alexander the Great** founds Alexandria, which becomes the capital of his Greek-speaking successors, the **Ptolemies**.

Augustus makes Egypt part of the **Roman Empire** in 30 B.C. Alexandria continues as provincial capital, but Augustus builds the fortress of Babylon, now in Old Cairo.

Christianity is introduced to Egypt in the first century A.D., and despite severe Roman persecution it takes root among Egyptians (*Aigyptoi* in Greek, from which **Copt** is derived). After A.D. 330 Egypt is ruled from Constantinople, capital of the Eastern Roman or **Byzantine Empire**.

In 632 **Muhammad**, the founder of Islam, dies in Arabia. Under his successors (caliphs) Arab armies invade Syria (636), Persia (637), and Egypt (640).

Greater Cairo

Key Places of Interest

1. Coptic Museum
2. Amr Mosque
3. Ibn Tulun Mosque
4. Citadel
5. Shagarat al-Durr Mausoleum
6. Imam al-Shafi Mausoleum
7. Aqueduct
8. Nilometer
9. Sultan Hasan and Rifai Mosques
10. Al-Azhar Park
11. Islamic Museum
12. Bab Zuwayla
13. Al-Azhar Mosque
14. Khan al-Khalili
15. Qalaun Mosque
16. Al-Hakim Mosque
17. Bab al-Futuh
18. Bab al-Nasr
19. Fatimid Wall
20. Saad Zaghloul Mausoleum
21. Ezbekiya Gardens
22. Manyal Palace
23. Opera House
24. Gezira Sporting Club
25. Cairo Tower
26. Egyptian Museum

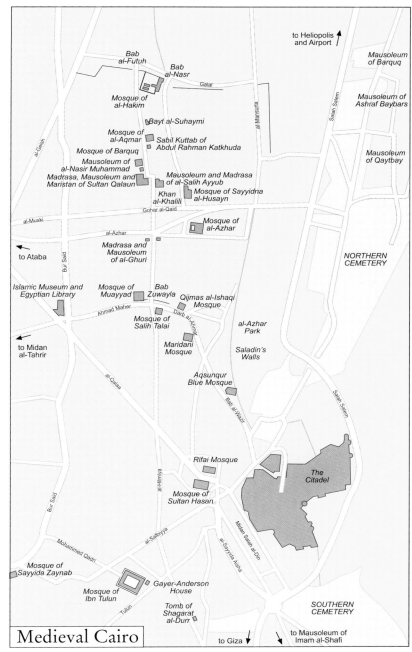

Medieval Cairo

Top left: A speedboat races along the river through Cairo, the banks of the Nile fringed with palms, skyscrapers, and traditional sailing boats called feluccas.

Bottom left: A great gift of the river, as here along this channel of the Nile between Roda and Old Cairo, is the mood of ease and peacefulness that makes it almost impossible to believe that you are in one of the world's largest and most crowded cities.

A.D. 642–1170: The Arab Settlements

In 642 the Arab general **Amr ibn al-As** builds the first mosque in Egypt outside the walls of Babylon and founds a new city, Fustat. Egypt becomes part of the Arab empire which at first is ruled from Medina in Arabia, then from 661 by the **Umayyad** dynasty in Damascus. In 725–26 the Copts revolt against the Arab occupation. In response the caliph in Damascus orders the first large-scale settlement of Arabs in Egypt.

After a violent transfer of dynasty in 750, the empire is ruled from Baghdad by the **Abbasids**.

In 870 **Ibn Tulun** (r. 870–84), the Abbasid governor of Egypt, makes himself independent of Baghdad and founds a new city, al-Qatai, north of Fustat.

The **Fatimids**, a North African Shia dynasty opposed to the Sunni Abbasid caliphate in Baghdad, invade Egypt in 969 and found al-Qahira (Cairo), with its al-Azhar Mosque, to the north of al-Qatai.

In 1055 the Islamic empire passes into non-Arab hands when the Seljuq Turks conquer Baghdad and assert their hegemony over the Sunni caliphate. The First Crusade captures Jerusalem in 1099. The

Right: Built more than 4,500 years ago, the Pyramid of Cheops, seen here from the gardens of the Mena House Hotel, remains the largest monument in the world. Like all pyramids, it was built to be the burial place of the pharaoh. According to ancient tradition a hundred thousand laborers, working three-month shifts, were involved in its construction, which took twenty years.

Modern calculations suggest, however, that only four thousand men would have been needed to work on the pyramid itself—more would merely have got in the way—and that these would have been highly skilled surveyors, masons, stone-cutters, and so on, employed year round. Others would have worked in the quarries, but the greatest number would have been unskilled peasants drawn from the land during the idle months when the Nile inundated the fields, and these would have done heavy tasks like dragging blocks to the site. None were compelled to work as slaves, and indeed graffiti found at the Great Pyramid of Cheops expresses the workers' delight in participating in such an extraordinary enterprise.

Fatimids destroy Fustat, which lies outside their walls, to deny it to the Crusaders, who attack Egypt in 1168.

1171–1798: Medieval Cairo

In 1171 the Fatimids are overthrown by **Saladin** (r. 1171–93) who installs himself as sultan, returns Egypt to Sunni Islam, and founds the **Ayyubid** dynasty. After building the Citadel and extending Cairo's walls, in 1187 he captures Jerusalem from the Crusaders.

In 1250 the Ayyubid sultans' slave army, called **Mamluks**, seizes power, its leaders ruling as sultans in turn. Among them are **Qalaun** (r. 1279–90), **al-Nasr** (r. 1309–40), **al-Hasan** (r. 1347–51, 1354–61), **Qaytbay** (r. 1468–95), and **al-Ghuri** (r. 1500–16), whose monuments adorn the city. During the reigns of al-Nasr and al-Hasan there are severe persecutions of Christians who until this time constitute half the population of Egypt, and mass conversions to Islam follow.

In 1517 the **Ottoman Turks** occupy Egypt, and Cairo, now a provincial city, declines.

From 1798: Modern Cairo

The brief French occupation of Egypt by **Napoleon**, from 1798 to 1801, gives Cairo its first whiff of western ways. Among the Ottoman officers sent to re-establish control over Egypt is **Muhammad Ali** (r. 1805–48), who soon makes himself ruler, drives forward the westernization of the country, and places his mark on the Cairo skyline with his mosque atop the Citadel. His grandson **Ismail** (r. 1863–79) lays out the pattern of streets and squares between the medieval city and the Nile that becomes the heart of modern Cairo.

To ensure the security of trade through the Suez Canal, the British occupy Egypt from 1882 to 1936, and British forces return to Egypt during World War II (1939–45) to repel the Germans and Italians.

In 1952 the monarchy is overthrown by army officers led by **Gamal Abd al-Nasser**. Today Greater Cairo, the largest city in Africa and the Arab world, has a population of eighteen million.

Below: Along with the Pyramids, the Mosque of Muhammad Ali atop the Citadel has come to symbolize Cairo.

7

Old Cairo

Old Cairo (*Masr al-Qadima* in Arabic) describes the area that grew up around the Roman **fortress of Babylon**, built in the time of Augustus after his conquest of Egypt in 30 B.C. In particular it is often taken to mean the settlement within the remains of the fortress itself, which surrendered to the Arabs in 641 and became known as *Qasr al-Shamah*, Fortress of the Beacon. Several ancient churches and a synagogue (generally open 8am–4pm daily) stand within or on the walls, some possibly built as early as the fourth century, though both Jews and Christians claim much older associations with the place.

At the southwest corner of the fortress, the **Coptic Church of al-Muallaqa**, the Hanging Church, was built on the bastions of the Roman gate, its nave suspended above the passage. The church

Above: The interior of the Hanging Church, with pointed arches, granite pillars, cedar paneling, and translucent ivory screens, is intricately decorated. The carved white marble pulpit inlaid with red and black marble is the finest in Egypt. Ancient icons show the Virgin and Child, and St. Mark, who according to tradition was the founder of Christianity in Egypt.

Left: The Coptic al-Muallaqa Church, meaning the Hanging Church, acquired its name because its nave is suspended across the tops of the bastions of a Roman gate.

Right: The Mari Girgis metro station at Old Cairo is only a few minutes' journey from central Cairo. In the background is a round Roman tower, one of two that flank the entrance to the gardens of the Coptic Museum. The Greek Orthodox Church of St. George (Mari Girgis) has been built into the tower, once part of the fortress of Babylon. The church and its adjacent monastery were originally established at Memphis but moved here when the ancient city was abandoned after the Arabs founded Fustat outside the walls of Babylon.

There is also a regular water-bus service along the Nile which puts in at the Mari Girgis dock. Departures are from the Maspero dock, about five hundred meters north of the Egyptian Museum.

may have begun as a small chapel for the soldiers at the gate, but the present structure, which in any case has been rebuilt, is unlikely to have been raised upon the walls until the Arab conquest made them redundant. Services are held in Arabic and also in Coptic, which nowadays is a liturgical language only but was once the everyday spoken language of Egyptians.

East of the church, steps lead down to a tunnel through which you enter the fortress precincts, a largely Coptic neighborhood of little winding streets with an almost rural atmosphere of remove. But times have not always been so peaceful. For security the churches usually avoided facing onto the street, and their main entrances were walled up against attack, so that entry was through a small side door in an otherwise blank façade.

Abu Sarga, the Coptic church of St. Sergius, is possibly the oldest church within the fortress; it is thought to date from the

Right: Along the lane leading past the Coptic Convent of Mari Girgis in Old Cairo.

Far right: Looking toward the Church of al-Adra, the Virgin, first built in the ninth century but destroyed and rebuilt in the eighteenth century. It is known also as Kasriyat al-Rihan, 'pot of basil,' a favored herb of the Greek Orthodox Church. The Fatimid caliph al-Hakim transferred it to Orthodox use because his mother was of that faith, but at his death it was restored to the Copts.

Below left: The tomb of a Christian family glimpsed from the lane leading to Abu Sarga.

Bottom right: To protect themselves from attack, churches often sealed their main doors, so that to enter Abu Sarga, the Church of St. Sergius, you must go down steps to pass through the small side door leading to the nave. Its crypt is said to have been a resting place of the Holy Family, a tradition founded on the biblical account of the Flight into Egypt: "The angel of the Lord appeareth to Joseph in a dream, saying, Arise, and take the young child and his mother, and flee into Egypt, and be thou there until I bring thee word: for Herod will seek the young child to destroy him." —*Matthew 2:13*

fourth or fifth century, though it was restored and partly rebuilt in the twelfth. Christian pilgrims from all over Europe visited Abu Sarga during the Middle Ages because of its associations with the Flight into Egypt; steps to the right of the altar lead down to the crypt where according to tradition the Holy Family found refuge after fleeing from Herod.

Farther along is the **Synagogue of Ben Ezra** whose neighborhood has gone away—Egypt's Jews were forced out of the country after the wars with Israel—but it can claim a more ancient history than anything else in Old Cairo. Ben Ezra is the oldest synagogue in Egypt and resembles an early Christian church. Indeed the Church of St. Michael did stand here from the fourth to ninth centuries, but the Copts had to sell it to the Jews to pay Ibn Tulun's tax toward the erection of his mosque. Possibly something of the original structure survives in the work undertaken by Abraham Ben Ezra, the Rabbi of Jerusalem, in the twelfth century. But Jews say the site has far older associations: in the sixth century B.C. Jeremiah preached here

after the destruction of Jerusalem under Nebuchadnezzar, and it was the presence of their community here, they say, that drew the Holy Family to Babylon. Also legend associates with this spot the story recounted in both the Bible and the Quran of the infant Moses being hidden among the bulrushes and discovered by the pharaoh's daughter as she strolled along the banks of the Nile. The synagogue has recently undergone extensive restoration, paid for by the Egyptian government and foreign donors.

Above: Sitt Barbara dates from the seventh century, and like Abu Sarga it was restored in Fatimid times. Both are typical of early Coptic churches in being basilicas with aisles separated from the nave by rows of columns which support a high timbered roof. St. Barbara, whose relics are in the church, was martyred in the third century when her father, discovering that she was a Christian, turned her over to the Roman authorities to be tortured and beheaded.

Bottom left: The carved wooden patterns on the altar screen in Sitt Barbara are typical of Coptic craftsmanship.

Bottom right: The Ark, like Ben Ezra Synagogue as a whole, displays Christian, Muslim, and Jewish decorative motifs.

Right: The majestic proportions of the synagogue are a reminder that by the twelfth century the Jews of this vicinity formed the most important Jewish community in Egypt, North Africa, Palestine, and Syria. Thousands of their books and documents were amassed in a hiding place, or *genizah*, within the synagogue, which was only rediscovered in the 1890s, when its treasures were distributed among several of the greatest libraries in world. They have since enabled scholars to piece together a remarkably detailed picture of medieval religious, commercial, and social life in Egypt, the Middle East, and throughout the Mediterranean.

The Coptic Museum

The exhibits in the **Coptic Museum** (open 9am–5pm daily; admission charge) cover the period when Christianity was the faith of the majority of Egyptians, from about A.D. 300 to 1000, and link the art of the pharaonic and Greco-Roman periods with that of Islam. The word Copt derives from *Aigyptoi*, the Greek for Egyptians, whom the Arab invaders in turn called *Qibt*.

The museum is arranged in sections, covering stonework, manuscripts, textiles, icons, and paintings as well as decorated ivories, woodwork, metalwork, pottery, and glass. The highest artistic achievement was in textiles, that most fragile and perishable of mediums, and so it is a special delight to be treated to such a quantity and variety of fine chemises, tapis, and clothes embroidered with saints and sacred symbols or graceful women and gazelles.

Beautifully carved wood ceilings and beams from old Coptic houses decorate the museum throughout, while wooden *mashrabiya* window screens, fixed together without glue or nails, admit a diffused light through their intricate Christian patterns.

Top left: Two towers of the fortress of Babylon mark the entrance to the Coptic Museum, pleasantly set in gardens near the Mari Girgis metro station. Built early in the twentieth century and recently renovated, the museum is a charming building, embracing green courtyards, airy and light within, its spirit in keeping with its collection.

Bottom left: Coptic art was the native art of Egypt and was expressed in both religious and secular terms. In its earliest forms it was pagan, and it is fascinating to see how Egyptians adapted pharaonic and Greco-Roman architectural and decorative elements to a new popular culture.

Above: This third- or fourth-century tapestry showing musicians and dancers is fluid, rhythmic, and beautifully observed. The Copts were at their best in textiles, blending plants, animals, birds, and human beings in sumptuous decorative patterns, a skill they developed from ancient Egyptian tradition, adding to it Greco-Roman and Sassanid (Persian) influences.

Right: A seventh-century apse painting from Bawit near Asyut in Upper Egypt, showing Mary and the Apostles, and above them Christ enthroned between the sun and moon and creatures of the Apocalypse.

Above: In the face of a Crusader attack in 1168, the Fatimids torched Fustat and withdrew into their walled palace city of Cairo to the north. Famine in 1200 further reduced the population, for the most part Copts and Jews, and Fustat fell into ruin.

Left: A community of earthenware makers has grown up amid the ruins of Fustat, their dwellings made of broken pots and other debris.

Right: Worshipers at the Amr Mosque.

Far right: The Mosque of Amr has been restored and expanded so often that nothing remains of the original mosque built here in 642, the first in Africa. A congregational mosque, its enormous courtyard was meant to accommodate all the faithful at prayers.

Fustat

A short walk north from the Roman towers of Babylon, and keeping the railway line on your left, brings you to the **Mosque of Amr**, beyond which lie the dismal **remains of Fustat**, once a brilliant and prosperous city. Both mosque and city owed their foundation to Amr ibn al-As, the Arab general to whom Babylon surrendered in 641 after he laid siege to it with fifteen thousand men. In the following year the invaders built a permanent camp outside the fortress walls which acquired the name Fustat, from the Greek *phossaton* or the Latin *fossatum*, meaning entrenchment. Though Amr wanted to retain Alexandria as the seat of government, he was ordered by the caliph at Medina to make Fustat the capital of conquered Egypt.

Fustat grew from an Arab garrison to the greatest emporium in the Islamic world, selling wares from as far as Spain and China, and famous for its luxury manufactures, especially glassware and ceramics. But the Fatimids burnt Fustat in 1168 rather than allow it to fall into the hands of their erstwhile ally, the Christian king of Jerusalem who was attempting to seize Egypt.

Today much of Fustat appears to be a vast and smoking rubbish dump. The curious should wander into its midst and be amazed and rewarded with one of the most fascinating sights in Cairo. Among the smoldering heaps is a community of **earthenware manufacturers** whose seemingly rubbish houses stand amid a complete and complex process for making fine clay and fashioning narghile stems, drums, small pots, large storage jars, and enormous drainage pipes—indeed these people meet the earthenware needs of a large part of Cairo. There are vats dug into the ground for mixing and refining clay, subterranean workshops where potters draw from shapeless lumps beautifully curved vessels with all the mastery and mystery of a fakir charming a snake, and there are enormous beehive kilns fired from below with mounds of wood shavings shoveled in by ash-blackened children.

The Mosque of Ibn Tulun
and the Gayer-Anderson House

In 868 Ahmad ibn Tulun was sent to Egypt as governor of Fustat by the Abbasid caliph in Baghdad. Within two years he had seized control of the entire country and by refusing to pay tribute to the caliph made himself the first ruler of an independent Egypt since Cleopatra. Ibn Tulun founded a new capital on higher ground to the northeast of densely populated Fustat. Called al-Qatai, meaning fiefs or wards, referring to the feudal allotments he granted within it to various groups of supporters, it was a pleasure city of palaces and spacious squares, and at its center was the awesome mosque that still bears his name.

But Ibn Tulun's dynasty was short-lived; his son Khumarawayh inherited his love of building but few of his other qualities. Suffering from insomnia, Khumarawayh laid out a pool of quicksilver surrounded by a loggia supported on silver columns, and here, rocked on the softest of couches, he courted sleep guarded by a blue-eyed lion. Encountering little opposition, the Abbasids restored their authority over Egypt in 905 and destroyed al-Qatai, sparing only the mosque, all that survives of the luxurious splendor of the Tulunid capital.

The **Mosque of Ibn Tulun** lies west of Midan Salah al-Din, the large square below the Citadel. The area is poor and rundown, but behind its outer walls the mosque achieves an isolation which heightens the dramatic effect of its bold simplicity. Built in 876–79, the mosque displays strong Mesopotamian influence, notably in being built of brick and for its strange spiral minaret, features imitated from the great mosque at Samarra where Ibn Tulun, the child of a Turkish slave, was raised.

A congregational mosque with an inner courtyard of parade-ground proportions, it strove to fulfill the ideal of accommodating

Top left: The Mosque of Ibn Tulun is the oldest intact and functioning Islamic monument in Cairo, and the largest mosque in the city.

Differing accounts are given of Ibn Tulun's decision to build his mosque of brick rather than of stone. One is that he expressed a wish not to rob Egypt's churches of their columns and was convinced when a Christian architect said that grandeur could be achieved by building with brick piers. Another is that Ibn Tulun, who was raised in Samarra, the court city of the Abbasids north of Baghdad, knew that the city had been built of red brick and covered in stucco as that allowed rapid construction over a vast area, precisely what he required for al-Qatai. Claims that Ibn Tulun borrowed stylistically from the Great Mosque at Samarra may be exaggerated; certainly the distinctive pointed arches of his mosque had already appeared in fourth-century Coptic churches.

Top right: Ibn Tulun's minaret with its external spiral staircase most likely owes its inspiration to the Samarra mosque whose minaret in turn was probably influenced by Mesopotamia's ancient ziggurats.

Right: Walking round the courtyard under the arcades allows you to appreciate the rhythm of the arches, the play of light and shadow, and the harmony of the ensemble.

all the troops and subjects of the city for Friday noon prayers. Arcades run round the inner courtyard on four sides, deeper along the *qibla* wall facing Mecca. Brick piers support the pointed arches which have a slight return, and the arches are decorated with carved stucco, a technique Ibn Tulun introduced to Egypt. The windows along the *qibla* wall have stucco grilles, permitting a faint light into this deeper arcade with its prayer niche or *mihrab* and beautifully carved pulpit or *minbar*, thirteenth-century restorations. The roof and some repairs to the stucco work are owed to twentieth-century restorers. Original, however, is the Quranic inscription carved in sycamore running at a height round the interior of the four arcades.

At the center of the courtyard is a thirteenth-century fountain. All these thirteenth-century restorations and additions were undertaken by the Mamluk sultan Lajin, who had murdered the incumbent sultan and hidden in the deserted mosque, recently used as a caravanserai: he vowed that if he survived to be raised to the sultanate he would restore his hideaway. He also rebuilt the minaret, giving it a squared base. You can climb the minaret right to the top, although as you round the spiral there is nothing to steady you and a high breeze adds to the vertigo. There is little close by but tenements with views into bedroom windows, though to the west you can see the Pyramids, to the north pick out the major landmarks of the Fatimid city, and below you contemplate the plan of the mosque.

At the southeast corner of the Ibn Tulun Mosque is Bayt al-Kritliya, the House of the Cretan Woman (in fact it is two houses knocked

Above: This carved stucco work on a pier by the *mihrab* in the Mosque of Ibn Tulun is thirteenth-century restoration work by Sultan Lajin.

Below: The effect as you enter the mosque courtyard is of severe simplicity, yet the details of carved stucco and sycamore and returning arches offer subtle relief.

Right: The Gayer-Anderson House in fact consists of two houses of the Ottoman period facing one another across a small alley; they are joined to one another by a bridge at an upper story.

Below: The reception hall in the Gayer-Anderson House. Women could gaze down upon guests from the screened galleries above. According to Lane in his 1830s book *Manners and Customs of the Modern Egyptians*, upper class women did not mind being kept apart from visitors in this way, rather "they generally look upon restraint with a degree of pride, as evincing the husband's care for them and value themselves upon their being hidden as treasures."

together, one sixteenth-century, the other seventeenth-century). It is better known as the **Gayer-Anderson House** (open 8am–4:30pm daily; admission charge), named after the British major who restored and occupied it during the first half of the twentieth century. He filled it with his eclectic collection of English, French, and oriental furniture and bric-a-brac, which gives the place a lived-in feeling.

Overlooking its large reception room is a balcony enclosed in a wooden *mashrabiya* screen from which the women of the harem could discreetly observe male visitors and their entertainments. Edward William Lane in his *Manners and Customs of the Modern Egyptians*, which describes Cairo in the 1830s, says that the women of Cairo "have the character of being the most licentious in their feelings of all females who lay any claim to be considered as members of a civilised nation. . . . What liberty they have, many of them, it is said, abuse; and most of them are not considered safe unless under lock and key, to which restraint few are subjected. It is believed that they possess a degree of cunning in the management of their intrigues that the most prudent and careful husband cannot guard against."

The Citadel

The great square in front of the Citadel, Midan Salah al-Din, was the gathering place for the annual pilgrimage to Mecca before it wound through the streets of Cairo and left the city through the northern gates of Bab al-Futuh and Bab al-Nasr. The long park to its south was a parade ground and polo field for the Mamluks. Up a ramp at the front of the Citadel is a gate, Bab al-Azab. The crooked lane behind the gate, enclosed by high walls, was the scene of the massacre of nearly five hundred Mamluks by Muhammad Ali in 1811. During the Ottoman occupation and even under Napoleon the Mamluks had survived and were a power to be reckoned with. Muhammad Ali consolidated his rule by inviting them to dinner at the Citadel, then bidding them homeward via this cul-de-sac and cutting them down with their bellies full.

Below: When the King of Jerusalem invaded Egypt in 1168, the Fatimids called on forces loyal to the Baghdad caliphate for help. Among them was a young Kurdish general called Saladin, who when the fighting was over stayed on as vizier. In 1171, however, he seized complete power and replaced the Fatimids with a dynasty of his own, known as the Ayyubids for his father Ayyub. In 1187 Saladin would drive the Crusaders out of Jerusalem itself, but before that he needed to ensure the defense of Cairo, which he accomplished by building the Citadel on a rocky spur of the Moqattam Hills.

The Bab al-Azab where Muhammad Ali slaughtered the Mamluks in 1811 is between the two round towers.

Right: The familiar dome and twin minarets of Muhammad Ali's mosque are visible from all over Cairo. Begun in 1824, construction was completed in 1848, a year before his death. In that time he established a dynasty and made Cairo the capital of a modernizing Egyptian state which was effectively independent of the Ottoman Empire. Muhammad Ali's body was finally placed within his mosque when its decorations were finished in 1857.

But the entrance to the Citadel is not on this west side, but on the eastern side off Salah Salem Street—a long counterclockwise walk or a taxi ride. The military still occupies part of the **Citadel** (open 8am–5pm daily; museums close at 4:30pm; admission charge), an echo of its role as the stronghold of the city from 1176 when Saladin built his fortress here to the reign of Muhammad Ali. For almost seven hundred years nearly all Egypt's rulers lived in the Citadel, and held court, dispensed justice, and received ambassadors here.

A succession of palaces and elaborate buildings thrown up during the Mamluk period were mostly leveled by Muhammad Ali when he built his mosque and palaces in their place, but a magnificent survival is the recently restored **Mosque of al-Nasr** dating from 1318–35. Once the principal mosque of the Citadel, it was built in the congregational style with an arcaded courtyard, many of the columns reused from pharaonic, Roman, and Byzantine buildings. Plain though it is outside, it is beautiful inside, all the more so as Selim, the

Ottoman conqueror of Egypt, stripped it of its marble panels which he shipped back to Constantinople, revealing its simple elegance.

Passing through the Bab al-Qullah, which is behind al-Nasr's Mosque, you enter the northern enclosure, where Mamluk troops were quartered and where military barracks are still found. Here are both the **Carriage Museum**, which includes a golden state carriage presented to Khedive Ismail by Napoleon III, and the **Military Museum**, its collection of weapons and costumes illustrating warfare in Egypt from ancient to modern times. Between al-Nasr's Mosque and the courtyard of Muhammad Ali's Mosque is the **Police Museum**, largely devoted to famous murders from pharaonic times to the present.

The **Mosque of Muhammad Ali**, which dominates the Cairo skyline, was built in 1824–48 in the style of an imperial Ottoman mosque, its half-domes buttresses for the high central dome and the two thin minarets adding an ethereal touch. You enter through a pretty forecourt with a fountain like a large Fabergé egg and a

Above: The Muhammad Ali Mosque is approached through a forecourt enclosed by the pleasing rhythm of columned and domed arcades.

Far left: A Turkish baroque fountain for ablutions stands at the center of the forecourt.

Left: This immense *minbar* or pulpit of gilded wood, used in the conduct of Friday prayers, is an original feature of the mosque.

Right: The vast interior of the Muhammad Ali Mosque is illuminated by great circular chandeliers suspended from the dome. The mosque's architect was a Greek who based his plans on the Blue Mosque in Constantinople.

gingerbread clock given by the French in exchange for the obelisk in the Place de la Concorde in Paris. But unfortunately the alabaster cladding here and elsewhere has discolored with time. The interior of the mosque is vast, the dome huge, and the decorations opulent, gigantic chandeliers illuminating the darkness with swirls of light.

Muhammad Ali, whose tomb is on the right as you enter, came to Egypt in 1801 with the Ottoman army which, together with the British, ejected the remnants of Napoleon's military expedition. An admirer of the West, Muhammad Ali devoted his energies to modernization, relying on European immigration, expertise, and capital to develop the country. Education was an important part of his development plan, and he established a system of government secondary schools and also sent students to Europe. These in turn

Above: The columns round the courtyard of the Mosque of al-Nasr were all taken from Ptolemaic, Roman, and Christian buildings as can be seen from their various capitals. This was the Citadel's principal place of worship until the construction of the Muhammad Ali Mosque whose dome and slender minarets can be seen behind.

Far left: The *mihrab* in the al-Nasr Mosque is covered by a dome supported on ten massive ancient Egyptian columns of red Aswan granite.

Left: The entrance to the al-Nasr Mosque is decorated with a typically Mamluk stalactite motif, but the minaret rising above it shows Persian inspiration in its chevron patterns and its fluted cap, still partly covered in green faience tiles.

became teachers, doctors, and engineers, the professional elite at the core of Egypt's new middle class. Muhammad Ali also promoted health reform and medical training. Doctors and midwives were educated in Egypt and many were sent to Europe to finish their training, returning to assume important posts in the expanding medical service. By the end of his reign he had transformed Egypt from an impoverished, disease-ridden, and stagnant backwater and had laid the foundations for a modern state.

You emerge from the mosque onto an open terrace with the **Bijou Palace** opposite. This was also built by Muhammad Ali and now serves as a museum, housing nineteenth-century royal portraits, costumes, and furnishings in its French-style salons.

From the southwest parapet of the terrace there is a good view of the mosques of Sultan Hasan and the Rifai and beyond them the great mosque of Ibn Tulun. The panorama of the city will be more or less impressive depending on the pollution.

The Southern Quarters

In the two thousand years since the death of Cleopatra, Egypt has known only one female ruler. Her name is **Shagarat al-Durr**, and to find her **tomb** you go a few hundred meters southward along the medieval city's main street, here called al-Khalifa Street, which passes just to the east of Ibn Tulun's mosque. The tomb stands behind iron railings at the edge of the Southern Cemetery in one of Cairo's poorest areas. Built in 1250, it is small and simple, though in allusion to her name, Tree of Pearls, the prayer niche inside bears fine Byzantine-style mosaics of the tree of life inlaid with mother-of-pearl.

In 1249, as the Seventh Crusade seized the Delta port of Damietta, Sultan al-Salih Ayyub was dying of cancer. But Shagarat al-Durr hid her husband's corpse and kept morale alive by pretending to transmit the sultan's orders to his army of Mamluk slave-troops. Meanwhile suffering in the heat, and fed bad fish by the Delta people, the Crusaders became sick with scurvy and plague, and they were easily

Left: The tomb of Shagarat al-Durr, whose name means Tree of Pearls. Of Armenian or Turkish stock, she shares with Hatshepsut and Cleopatra that rare distinction of having been a female ruler of Egypt. Al-Salih Ayyub purchased her as a slave and made her one of his concubines, though he would obligingly lend her out to friends; but when he became sultan he married her. Her resourcefulness and courage at her husband's death saved Egypt from the Seventh Crusade, and afterward she declared herself sultan, basing her claim to the succession on having borne al-Salih a son, though the child had predeceased his father. In fact her tomb probably contains very little of Shagarat al-Durr; at the end she was thrown over the Citadel walls and her body was left to the dogs.

Below left: The Sabil Kuttab of Sultan Qaytbay stands along the street running between Ibn Tulun's mosque and the Citadel, which marks the northern limit of the Southern Cemetery. A *sabil* or public fountain topped by a *kuttab* or Quranic school for boys was a Mamluk innovation, of which this is a particularly richly decorated example.

Below right: The Southern Cemetery is inhabited by the living as well as by the dead. Washing is strung across a street leading to the mausoleum of Zayn al-Din Yusuf, the leader of a Sufi brotherhood who died in 1297.

Below right: The mausoleum of Imam al-Shafi is the largest Islamic mortuary chamber in Egypt. Saladin built a *madrasa* complex on the spot, now replaced by a nineteenth-century mosque, and placed a cenotaph over the imam's grave, while Saladin's nephew al-Khalil built the burial chamber itself. Another holy man, Sayyid Muhammad Abd al-Hakam, is buried adjacent to the imam, and two other cenotaphs mark the burial places of Sultan al-Khalil and his mother. The mausoleum is a popular shrine; women come to pray, men sit and read the Quran, cats wander in and out, and birds chirp high within the colorful and airy dome. The original lighting system of lamps suspended from carved beams is intact, the only such example in Cairo.

Below left: Atop the dome of the imam's mausoleum is a metal boat in which about a hundred and fifty kilos of wheat and a camel-load of water for the birds used to be placed on the occasion of the *moulid*. The boat is said to turn sometimes when there is no wind to move it, and according to the position it takes to foretoken various events, good or evil: plenty, scarcity, or the death of some great man.

routed in battle. In May 1250 Shagarat al-Durr openly proclaimed herself sultan, but the Abbasid caliph refused to recognize her. So she married one of her Mamluk slave-warriors and ruled through him instead until his interest wandered. In 1257 she murdered him in his bath. His supporters killed her and threw her naked body over the Citadel walls to be devoured by dogs. As the widow of al-Salih Ayyub, Shagarat al-Durr was the last of the Ayyubid dynasty founded by Saladin, and at her death the Mamluks made themselves masters of Egypt.

The Southern Cemetery is a vast, confusing, and dilapidated Muslim necropolis, all the more strange because it is very much inhabited by the living. But finding your way to the **mausoleum of Imam al-Shafi** more than repays the effort. The mausoleum is most easily reached by heading south from the Citadel along the street bearing the imam's name, a distance of about two kilometers from Midan Salah al-Din. A descendant of an uncle of the Prophet Muhammad, al-Shafi was the founder of one of the four rites of

Above: The Mamluk aqueduct was built to bring water from the Nile to the Citadel.

Far left: A footbridge crosses over a narrow channel of the Nile from Old Cairo to the southern tip of Roda.

Left: There has probably been a Nilometer at the southern end of Roda since ancient times, but the present Nilometer dates from 861, while its superstructure with its Turkish-style conical roof dates from Muhammad Ali's reign.

Sunni Islam and died in 820. Later Saladin founded the first *madrasa* in Egypt on this spot to counter the Shia teachings of the Fatimids, and his nephew al-Kamil added within the complex a beautiful tomb chamber for the imam. The mausoleum is annually the site of a great *moulid*, an anniversary birthday festival in his honor.

The Mamluk **aqueduct** passes through these southern quarters. On the Nile corniche opposite the island of Roda there is a traffic roundabout called Fumm al-Khalig: mouth of the Khalig. This is where an ancient canal left the river, and it is also the starting point of the aqueduct. The octagonal stone tower by the roundabout once housed great waterwheels which lifted water from the Nile to the level of the Mamluk aqueduct that can still be followed almost all the way to the Citadel. The section of the aqueduct nearest the river dates only from 1505; the main part of the aqueduct, farther east, was built by al-Nasr around 1311.

The lower end of Roda island lies opposite Old Cairo, and a footbridge connects the two. At the southern tip of the island is the **Nilometer** (open 9am–5pm daily; admission charge), the oldest surviving Islamic monument in Cairo, its purpose to determine the agricultural fertility of Egypt each year.

Right: At the center of the Nilometer's stone-lined pit is a graduated column for determining whether the river would rise enough, not enough, or too much, so announcing the expected fertility of all Egypt over the coming year. A reading of 16 ells (8.6 meters) ensured the complete irrigation of the valley; then the Nile crier would broadcast the *Wafa al-Nil* or superfluity of the Nile, and the dam to the Khalig would be cut amid great festivity. The Nile used to reach its flood at Cairo in mid-August, but the High Dam at Aswan now regulates its flow and it keeps a fairly constant level year-round.

The Sultan Hasan and Rifai Mosques

Facing the Citadel across Midan Salah al-Din are two large mosques pressed against each other like the walls of a canyon, the pedestrianized al-Qalaa Street cutting between them. The mosque to the northeast is the **Rifai**, built in the late nineteenth and early twentieth centuries in Mamluk style, where members of the late royal family, including Khedive Ismail and King Farouk are buried, as well as the last shah of Iran who died in exile in Cairo.

Opposite is the **Mosque of Sultan Hasan**, genuinely of the Mamluk period and built on a stupendous scale in 1356–63, reputedly of stone from the Pyramid of Cheops. There are many who regard the mosques of Sultan Hasan and of Ibn Tulun as the outstanding Islamic monuments in Egypt. Though entirely different in type, the two mosques share a boldness of conception and clarity of execution, gathering still more strength in restraining decoration to the minimum necessary solely to underline architectural form.

Unlike congregational mosques such as the Ibn Tulun, where the purpose was to gather all the faithful, the Mosque of Sultan Hasan served as a *madrasa*, that is a theological school, an institution first introduced to Egypt by Saladin to extirpate the Shia doctrines of the Fatimids and instill Sunni orthodoxy in their place. The need to accommodate classrooms and dormitories at least partly explains the

Above: Ablutions are performed at the canopied fountain in the courtyard of the Sultan Hasan Mosque. On festival days the fountain was filled with sherbet.

Below: The courtyard is surrounded by *iwans*, immense vaulted recesses originally meant as places for teaching.

Right: The dark entrance passage opens onto the central courtyard, which is of considerable depth, its *iwan*s lifting about as high as the courtyard is long, so that it is rarely entirely filled by the sun.

Bottom left: The monumental scale of the Sultan Hasan Mosque is emphasized by the towering entrance portal with its stalactite decorations, a favorite Mamluk motif.

Bottom right: The view toward the Citadel with the Rifai Mosque on the left and the Mosque of Sultan Hasan on the right. The projection above the entrance portal of the Sultan Hasan Mosque once supported a minaret which fell in 1361, shortly before Hasan's disappearance, killing over three hundred people.

towering bulk of the Sultan Hasan Mosque. Four enormous vaulted halls or *iwans* open on to each side of its central courtyard, each *iwan* serving as a place for teaching one of the four rites of Sunni Islam.

To the left and right of the *mihrab* are doors leading into the mausoleum. The right-hand door is paneled with original bronze inlaid with gold and dazzles when polished. The mausoleum dome collapsed in the seventeenth century and was rebuilt in the eighteenth century in the lofty imperial style of Constantinople, though it rests on the original stalactite squinches. Rich though the restored decorations are, the atmosphere is somber and Hasan's cenotaph, surrounded by a wooden screen where women pray for the sultan's intercession, is very simple. Cenotaph or not, the sultan's tomb is empty; he was murdered two years before the completion of his mosque and his body disappeared.

Above: Women keep to the background during prayers in the sanctuary *iwan* facing Mecca. The monumental stucco inscription running along the upper wall tells of the mercy of Allah and the paradise awaiting the faithful.

Left: The *mihrab* is intricately inlaid with colored marble. On either side are columns taken from some Christian edifice, probably a Crusader church.

Right: The Muhammad Ali Mosque atop the Citadel as seen through the grilled windows of the Rifai Mosque.

Far right: The cenotaph for King Farouk in the Rifai Mosque. His body is buried nearby beneath some slabs of marble flooring. His father King Fuad and grandfather Khedive Ismail are also interred at the Rifai.

Above: The Citadel View Restaurant occupies the high ground in the park.

Left: The loggia in the restaurant's upper story offers magnificent panoramas over Cairo throughout the day and evening.

Right: The view toward the Citadel is enlivened by a succession of water features.

Far Right: The park overlooks the Darb al-Ahmar, a neighborhood rich in Islamic architecture which is being regenerated as part of the Aga Khan's project.

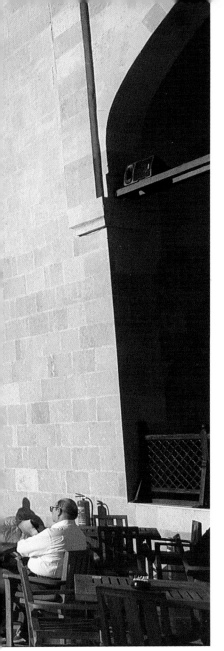

Al-Azhar Park

The entrance to **al-Azhar Park** (open 10am–12 midnight; admission charge) is on Salah Salem Street about half a kilometer from al-Azhar Street as you head toward the Citadel. Inaugurated in 2005, the park stands on high ground and enjoys commanding views over the medieval quarters of Cairo and the City of the Dead. The play of sparkling fountains, waterfalls, and pools set amid an undulating landscape of lawns, palms, sycamores, blackthorns, and acacias is reminiscent of the grandeur and mystery of the gardens of Andalusia.

The park is the creation of the Aga Khan Trust for Culture. As the spiritual leader of the world's Ismaili Muslims, whose faith is that of the Fatimid founders of Cairo, the Aga Khan is keen to see the park work as a catalyst for economic, social, and cultural renewal, especially in the neighboring Darb al-Ahmar area. Al-Azhar Park is also meant as a step toward the ecological rehabilitation of Cairo generally, which has one of the lowest ratios of green space to urban population in the world, working out to about a footprint per inhabitant.

In fact there was a park here in Fatimid times, but later the site became a rubbish dump. Five hundred years worth of rubble and debris, amounting to eighty thousand truckloads, had to be removed. Then three large reservoirs for providing Cairo with fresh water were sunk into the spot, and the entire area was landscaped and planted with hundreds of thousands of specially grown plants and trees. In the process a one-and-a-half kilometer section of all-but-buried Ayyubid wall was excavated, its towers, gates, and battlements now revealed in all their splendor along the western boundary of the park.

From its Moorish-style hilltop restaurant to its charming lakeside pavilion, al-Azhar Park offers marvelous panoramas across Cairo's historic quarters and is drawing tourists and Cairenes alike to this once-neglected area.

Darb al-Ahmar

Darb al-Ahmar is the neighborhood to the west of al-Azhar Park from which it is separated by a kilometer and a half's length of Ayyubid wall with crenellations and towers. Until the fourteenth century the quarter had been Fatimid and Ayyubid cemeteries extending south from Bab Zuwayla and the Fatimid city. The area became fashionable during the Mamluk period, however, and it has many fine monuments which date from that time, and in the nineteenth century it became a prosperous residential area. But throughout the twentieth century Darb al-Ahmar declined, so that its name has come to epitomize a poor and broken-down part of the city. In recent years, and in large part due to the stimulus generated by the development of al-Azhar Park, Darb al-Ahmar has been undergoing an extensive and culturally sensitive rehabilitation program.

Darb al-Ahmar takes its name from a section of the long street which curves northward from the Citadel toward the Fatimid city. It begins as al-Mahga Street which issues from the northeast end of Midan Salah al-Din; then, as Bab al-Wazir Street, the street of the Gate of the Vizier, it plunges downhill through the quiet residential area of the quarter; and finally, as it enters the livelier bazaar area toward Bab Zuwayla, it is called Darb al-Ahmar, the Red Road. Along the way are many old houses and some fine monuments, some dilapidated, even ruinous, others being restored.

The pleasure of Darb al-Ahmar is the slow walk and the occasional pause along the way, noting a carved window projecting over the street or some other fine remnant of domestic architecture, and

Above: Setting off down Bab al-Wazir Street from near the Citadel.

Below: Drying the washing and doing the shopping from a projecting window in the Darb al-Ahmar quarter.

Above: South of the Blue Mosque, the Mosque of Atymish, built in 1383, is recognized by its dome with slanting ribs.

Right: The delicacy of the Ottoman tiles in the Blue Mosque is in contrast to the boldness of its Mamluk form.

Below left: The entirety of the *qibla* wall of the Mosque of Aqsunqur is covered with blue tiles made in Ottoman factories in Damascus. The floral motif flanked by cypresses is in shades of blue, green, and turquoise—the predominance of blues accounting for the popular name of Blue Mosque. Aqsunqur was a commander under Sultan al-Nasr but was strangled by one of the sultan's sons.

Below right: A shop in Bab al-Wazir Street.

Far left: A grocer amid his produce.

Left: This doorway of a newly refurbished house in Darb al-Ahmar has been marked with the hands of children dipped in blood to ward away the evil eye of envy. The handprints were made during the moulid of Fatma al-Nabawiya, a relative of the Prophet Muhammad, when as an act of piety a local man, a prosperous carpenter, sacrifices two buffalos or cows in the street.

Bottom: A tire shop in Darb al-Ahmar; its name is a colloquial expression meaning 'I'm satisfied with what I have.'

Right: These two domes and minaret built in 2004 in Mamluk revival style mark the tomb complex of Fatma al-Nabawiya who is credited with powers to cure the mentally retarded. One of the best moulids in Egypt is held in the streets of Darb al-Ahmar each year in her honor, with pilgrims coming from as far off as the Delta and Upper Egypt. Moulids, which are like raucous street festivals with music and snake charmers, are some of the few occasions on which people can act without inhibitions, and the moulid of Fatma al-Nabawiya in particular is a time when people dress up in strange costumes covered with prayer beads, charms, and jewelry, and men and also women dance in the streets.

visiting the mosques which are still very much places of community worship rather than tourist sights.

Soon after setting off down Bab al-Wazir Street you come on your right to the **Mosque of Aqsunqur**, which is undergoing fitful restoration. It is popularly known as the **Blue Mosque** for its tiles, brought from Damascus by the Ottoman governor of Cairo in 1652, though the mosque itself is Mamluk and dates from 1347. The crudely carved pillars round the courtyard and the stand of trees at its center give the mosque an agreeably rustic touch. On the left before entering the courtyard is the tomb of Sultan Kuchuk, the Little One, a son of Sultan al-Nasr who ruled for five months at the age of six, but was then deposed, imprisoned in the Citadel, and three years later strangled by an older brother.

Behind the Aqsunqur Mosque and clearly visible from the street is a section of Saladin's walls, while across the street from the mosque is a Turkish apartment building from 1625.

Continuing north, soon after Bab al-Wazir Street becomes Darb al-Ahmar, is the **Maridani Mosque**, set at an angle on the left side of the street. Built in 1339–40 in the early Mamluk period, it is one of the oldest buildings in the quarter. Entering from the bustle of the street you are soon absorbed into the restfulness of the mosque. An easy rhythm of arches on slender antique columns, their capitals taken from pharaonic, classical, and Byzantine buildings, runs round the courtyard. A wooden screen separates the *qibla* arcade from the courtyard, a unique feature in Cairo. The *mihrab* is beautifully decorated with mosaic and the dome above it is supported by several columns of red Aswan granite. Before leaving, climb up the minaret for a good view of the medieval city.

Far left: A formerly Jewish residence in Darb al-Ahmar, its gateway bearing the Star of David.

Left: Veiled woman and screened windows in Darb al-Ahmar.

Above: Looking across the tree-filled courtyard of the Maridani Mosque toward the *qibla* arcade, its dome supported by pharaonic columns. Maridani, like his fellow amir Aqsunqur, was a son-in-law of Sultan al-Nasr who encouraged them to build mosques and contributed materials.

Right: The *qibla* arcade is separated from the courtyard of the Maridani Mosque by a finely worked *mashrabiya* screen. Though the screen has been restored, the basic fabric is original, the wood preserved in the dry air of Cairo.

43

The Islamic Museum

Above: A hexagonal Quran table, dating to the early fourteenth century, finely crafted of copper and inlaid with silver.

A visit to the **Islamic Museum** (Midan Ahmed Maher at the intersection of al-Qalaa and Port Said Streets; open 9am–3pm daily; admission charge), which lies to the west of Bab Zuwayla, will enhance your understanding and appreciation of the Islamic monuments in the medieval city.

The museum, which has recently received a complete overhaul, presents exhibits representing twelve hundred years of Islamic art and does so chronologically for the most part as you move through a succession of large, airy, and well-lit rooms.

The art of the Umayyad period (seventh–eighth centuries) was representational and drew on Hellenistic and Persian sources.

Abbasid (eighth–tenth centuries) and Tulunid works (from the ninth–tenth centuries) show greater stylization, with the emphasis on decoration rather than representation, and with great use of stucco, characterized by its slant cut.

The Fatimids (tenth–twelfth centuries), who were Shia, did not observe the Sunni prohibition on representation of higher living forms, and were much influenced by the Persians, whose craftsmen they imported. The museum contains some very fine examples of Fatimid woodwork, carved with human and animal figures and foliage. A carved frieze, originally from the western Fatimid palace (tenth century), shows scenes of hunting, music, and other courtly activities rarely found in Islamic art.

The Ayyubid period (twelfth–thirteenth centuries) is well represented by fine wood, marble, and stucco carving.

Among the outstanding works of the Mamluk period (thirteenth–sixteenth centuries) there is a magnificent fourteenth-century lantern of bronze chased with silver from the Sultan Hasan Mosque. Despite the bloody succession of Mamluk sultans, Egypt during much of this period enjoyed peace and the decorative arts flourished. A Chinese influence was felt in Mamluk ceramics and pottery. Soft woods were inlaid with ivory, bone, tin, and ebony, usually in star-polygons, and arabesque floral designs found favor.

From the Ottoman period (sixteenth–eighteenth centuries) are magnificent *mashrabiya*s, wooden screens which preserved the privacy of the house from the gaze of the street while still admitting refreshing breezes. They were also used to screen off interior harem rooms from courtyards and reception halls. Also there are windows of openwork plaster filled with colored glass, and tapestries, china, jewelry, and enameled glass lamps.

Top: Painted in blue, green, red, and black, this tile panel displays the Kaaba in Mecca and was used to decorate a *qibla* wall.

Above: Found in a storeroom of the mosque of Sayyida Zaynab, this wooden door is decorated with a silver medallion at its center.

Above right: A gold and silver inlaid rosewater sprinkler made for Sultan Hasan's mosque.

Right: The façade of the Islamic Museum in Cairo.

From Bab Zuwayla to al-Azhar

When the Fatimids conquered Egypt in 969 they built their walled royal city to the north of Fustat and al-Qatai, and in honor of their caliph named it al-Qahira al-Muizziya, City of al-Muizz's Victory. In time the name was simplified to al-Qahira, that is Cairo, and was applied to everything both within and without the walls. Nothing of the Fatimids' luxurious palaces and pavilions has survived, but Bab Zuwayla, their city's formidable southern gate built in 1092, still stands as a reminder of their magnificence and power.

Facing the square in front of Bab Zuwayla, the **Mosque of al-Salih Talai**, built toward the end of the Fatimid period in 1160, is one of the most handsome in Cairo. A lower level of shops was part of the mosque's *waqf* or endowment, the rents contributing to its upkeep. The five keel-arches of the façade, supported by classical columns linked by wooden tie-beams, form a porch which is unique in the city.

Below: The handsome keel-arch porch of the Mosque of al-Salih Talai faces on to the small square outside Bab Zuwayla, near the covered Street of the Tentmakers. Al-Salih Talai was an Armenian and a governor of Upper Egypt from where he was summoned to put down disturbances in Cairo. Six years later he was poisoned by a princess, whom he had executed before him as he died.

Right: Bab Zuwayla, the massive southern gate into the Fatimid city, was built by an Armenian vizier to the caliph. The annual pilgrimage to Mecca passed this way, sultans rode by in ceremonial processions, and captive prisoners were led through the gate in chains. Public executions took place here, the severed heads and crucified bodies displayed on the gate. Tumanbay, the last Mamluk sultan, was hanged here by the Ottomans. Twice the rope broke before it did its work.

Bottom left and right: Keel-arches and tie-beams, which are characteristic of Fatimid architecture, impress their graceful rhythm on the Mosque of al-Salih Talai.

Top far left: Bab Zuwayla was named after the al-Zawila, a Berber tribe whose Fatimid soldiery were quartered nearby. But most inhabitants know it as Bab al-Mitwalli after al-Kutb al-Mitwalli, a nineteenth-century Muslim saint with healing powers, who is said to make his presence known by a gleam of light mysteriously appearing behind the west door.

Top left: The house of Gamal al-Din al-Dahabi with its *mashrabiya* window overhanging a side street off Muizz was the home of the foremost gold merchant in seventeenth-century Cairo.

Bottom left: The *sabil* or fountain of Muhammad Ali stands above a vast reservoir with sufficient capacity to provide Cairenes with one and a half million cups of water.

Below: Employing marble and timber imported from Turkey, the *sabil* was built in an Ottoman interpretation of European baroque that was very modern at the time. The façade is decorated with calligraphic verses extolling the gift of water by Muhammad Ali.

Along with Bab al-Futuh and Bab al-Nasr to the north, **Bab Zuwayla** is one of the three surviving gates of the sixty that once encircled medieval Cairo and which, well into the nineteenth century, were locked at night. There are wonderful views from the elegant minarets springing from the massive towers of Bab Zuwayla; they belong to the **Mosque of Muayyad**, built in 1416–20, its entrance just within the gate.

A short distance farther north and on the right where the street makes a small wiggle is the ornate Ottoman-style **Sabil of Muhammad Ali**, a public fountain built by Egypt's ruler in 1820 in honor of his son Tusun, who had died of plague. Recently and magnificently restored, the *sabil* can be visited, including the huge underground cistern from which it drew four thousand cups of water a day.

Continuing up to the intersection with the modern al-Azhar Street, you come on the left to the **Mosque of al-Ghuri**, the penultimate Mamluk sultan. A keen polo player into his seventies, a grandiose

Right: The cruciform interior of the mosque-*madrasa* of al-Ghuri. It is the last great architectural work of the Mamluks before the Ottoman invasion of Egypt; indeed al-Ghuri himself died in battle against the Ottomans at Aleppo in Syria.

Below: Looking along Muizz Street from the al-Ghuri Mosque to Bab Zuwayla. Muizz Street also runs north to Bab al-Futuh, and throughout its length from one gate to the other it enjoys successive traditional names, each one demarcating a souk reserved to a particular trade. Outside the al-Ghuri Mosque it was Suq al-Harir, the silk souk.

Bottom left: In Muizz Street one of the few tarboosh makers left in Cairo survives on sales to tourists and big hotels.

Bottom right: A pavement café along al-Azhar Street.

49

builder, an arbitrary despot, a torturer, murderer, and thief, indeed everything you would expect a Mamluk sultan to be, he inaugurated his mosque-*madrasa* in May 1503 with a great banquet attended by the Abbasid caliph and all the principal civil, military, and religious officials, the souks down to Bab Zuwayla magnificently illuminated and decorated.

A hundred meters east of al-Ghuri's mosque is the famous **Mosque of al-Azhar**, 'the most blooming.' Completed in 972, it was the first mosque built by the Fatimids in their city, and is the world's oldest university and foremost center of Islamic theology. Al-Azhar's religious curriculum has remained unchanged since the days of Saladin, who suppressed its Shia teachings and made al-Azhar the home of Sunni doctrine, though in 1961 Nasser obliged the university to include schools of medicine, science, and foreign languages, so that in many ways it is now competitive with other institutions of higher education in Egypt. The modern university buildings are behind the mosque proper.

Left: Al-Azhar Mosque was built in 972, but the picturesque minarets and domes with their fairytale effect were added in Mamluk times.

Above: You enter al-Azhar Mosque through the double-arched Gate of the Barbers where new students had their heads shaved. The gilded and enameled decoration dates from the mid-eighteenth century when the mosque was greatly restored.

Right: The courtyard of the mosque retains its original Fatimid features. The columns round the arcades are all different and were taken mostly from early churches.

Khan al-Khalili

In the fourteenth century when Cairo stood at the center of the highly profitable East–West trade in spices and other luxury goods, Garkas al-Khalili, Sultan Barquq's master of horse, acquired the old Fatimid royal cemetery that was on this spot, dug up the bodies, dumped them in the rubbish heaps outside the city walls, and in 1382 built his new *khan* on the site.

Foreign merchants were immediately attracted to the stalls of tradesmen and artisans which sprang up all around, forming the vast commercial quarter of covered streets and lanes which takes its name from the original Khan al-Khalili.

Lively throughout the day and well into the night, **Khan al-Khalili** is nowadays a tourist bazaar, selling everything from souvenirs to antiques. The importuning is relentless, but there is atmosphere and adventure all the same.

Left: Sikket al-Badestan, the main street through Khan al-Khalili, runs west from the Mosque of Sayyidna al-Husayn, a modern structure with slender Turkish-style minarets. The square outside the mosque is the scene of popular nightly celebrations throughout the month of Ramadan.

Above: Fishawi's is a famous old café just off Midan Sayyidna al-Husayn. It has been open every day and night for over two hundred years.

Right: Muski glass, recognizable by its numerous air bubbles, has been handblown in Cairo since the Middle Ages.

Following pages: The Badestan at the center of Khan al-Khalili; it was traditionally used to house the most precious wares because it could be locked and guarded at night.

53

The Heart of Medieval Cairo

Muizz Street, which runs between Bab Zuwayla and Bab al-Futuh, was the principal thoroughfare of al-Qahira, the Cairo of the Fatimids. Where it now presses its way along the western edge of Khan al-Khalili, it was once a broad avenue, so broad that it served as a parade ground, with the great palaces of the Fatimids looming like mountains, it was said, on either side. Throughout the Fatimid and the Mamluk periods, this was the very heart of Cairo, and there is still enough mystery and beauty to remind you that this was the original city of *A Thousand and One Nights*.

Looking north along Muizz Street you see on the west side the splendid cluster of domes and minarets that are the **Madrasas and Mausoleums of Qalaun**, of his son and successor **al-Nasr**, who built the aqueduct and the mosque at the Citadel, and of **Barquq**. Qalaun was one of the ablest, most successful, and long-lived (1220–90) of

Right: Looking north along Muizz Street with the minaret of Qalaun's mosque in the far distance. The street is narrow and humble now, but in the days of the Fatimids it was the width of a parade ground, and royal palaces towered on either side. Mamluk sultans made their triumphal entries along this street, led by singers and poets celebrating their conquests and the achievements of their reigns. Amid fluttering banners of silk and gold the sultan would appear, a parasol of yellow silk held above his head, surmounted with a golden cupola on which perched a golden bird. A band of flutes and trumpets, of kettledrums and hautboys, brought up the rear, their music mingling with the clamor of the street.

Top left: There has been a spice market on Muizz Street since Fatimid times. The commerce with Europe in Eastern spices reached its height in the Mamluk period.

Bottom left: Where it passes along the western side of Khan al-Khalili, Muizz is known as the Street of the Coppersmiths where everything from simple pots to elaborate finials to place atop mosques is made and sold.

Below: In a continuity of Cairene architecture, this *sabil* or fountain of the early Ottoman period reproduces the joggled architrave that was a feature of Mamluk decoration.

the notoriously short-lived Mamluk sultans, and moreover founded a dynasty lasting nearly a hundred years. Brought as a slave to Cairo from the steppes north of the Caucasus by the amir Aqsunqur, whose Blue Mosque is in Darb al-Ahmar, Qalaun served the country of his purchase well: Damascus and Baghdad had fallen to the Mongols but Qalaun beat them back and then marched against the Crusaders at Acre, their last stronghold in the Holy Land. An outstanding builder, his tribute to his Christian enemies was the adoption of Gothic elements in his complex here.

Across the street from Qalaun's buildings is the **Madrasa and Mausoleum of al-Salih Ayyub**, the last ruler of Saladin's dynasty. He began the practice of buying Mamluk slaves from the Caucasus and lower Volga region to serve as his bodyguard. His wife was Shagarat al-Durr, the Tree of Pearls, who briefly ruled as sultan in her own right before the Mamluks took over Egypt for themselves.

Above: The façade of the domed mausoleum built for al-Salih Ayyub by his widow Shagarat al-Durr.

Below: The Mosque and Madrasa of Qalaun seen from the east. You can visit the house of Uthman Katkhuda, a fine example of Mamluk domestic architecture, which is the tall house along the row of buildings on the right.

These buildings of Qalaun, al-Nasr, and Barquq were built over the central part of the Fatimids' western palace, while al-Salih Ayyub's *madrasa* and mausoleum marks the center of the eastern palace. The two palaces were staffed by twelve thousand domestics. They covered an area of 400,000 square meters, and from al-Azhar Street to the south they extended well over half a kilometer northward to the Mosque of Aqmar. The Fatimids, like the Mamluks, ruled Egypt not as a province but as an independent state, and raised Cairo to prosperity and glory.

On a triangular plot at a fork in Muizz Street stands the charming **Sabil Kuttab of Abdul Katkhuda**. Built in 1744, the *kuttab*, whose porches overhang the roadways on either side, still serves as the

Right: This great marble Gothic arch set in the façade of Qalaun's *madrasa* is in fact a magnificent piece of booty, taken by his son and successor, al-Ashraf Khalil, from the Church of St. Andrew at Acre after its capture in 1291 and placed facing the street for all to see, a reminder to the Mamluks' subjects of the triumph of Islam over the Crusaders.

Below: Joggled Mamluk decoration round a doorway in the Madrasa of al-Nasr.

Bottom left: Minarets loom over the *iwan* in al-Nasr's *madrasa*.

Bottom center: Al-Nasr's minaret has a finely carved stucco surface.

Bottom right: The stucco decoration of Qalaun's minaret, like that of al-Nasr's, is probably the work of North African or Andalusian craftsmen.

Left: The view south along Muizz Street toward the complexes of Barquq, al-Nasr, and Qalaun. The scene is still that of *A Thousand and One Nights*, ostensibly set in Baghdad, though Baghdad by then had been razed by Tamerlane and it was the Cairo of the Mamluks that was described.

Below left: The Sabil Kuttab of Abdul Katkhuda.

Below right: The entrance portal to the Mosque of al-Aqmar, the first to have a decorated façade, and one of the few Fatimid mosques to have survived intact.

Bottom: A street seller by the Sabil of Ismail Pasha, built in the Ottoman style by Muhammad Ali in honor of one of his sons.

neighborhood Quaranic school. Below it is faced with the great grille of what was the *sabil*. Eminent Cairenes built not only for Allah or themselves, but also for the community, and a *sabil* or public watering fountain was often provided. This was in keeping with Prophet Muhammad's reply when asked what was the most meritorious act: "To give people water to drink."

Following the left-hand fork shortly brings you, on the right, to the **Mosque of al-Aqmar**, a rare survival of Fatimid architecture in this Mamluk-dominated part of the city. *Aqmar* means 'moonlit': it was so named for its pale stone. Built in 1125, the mosque façade is the oldest in Cairo and displays a typically Fatimid keel-arch portal. The niche ribbing, used here for the first time, was to become a favorite Cairo motif. The mosque was originally sited at the northeast corner of the eastern palace of the Fatimids, since when the level of the street has risen dramatically, which is why you must descend stairs in order to enter.

Bayt al-Suhaymi

Built in the sixteenth and seventeenth centuries, **Bayt al-Suhaymi** is a merchant's house of the Ottoman period—a description which, like its blank façade along Harat al-Darb al-Asfar, a narrow street running east off Muizz Street, hardly prepares you for what lies within. This is one of the finest houses in Cairo and wonderfully achieves the ambition of Islamic secular architecture—the anticipation of paradise.

The house (open daily 9am–6pm; admission charge) consists of numerous rooms on irregular levels, *mashrabiya* screen windows looking out onto the streets at one side, screened and latticed windows and arched galleries giving onto a garden courtyard on the other. In this way prosperous Cairenes defeated heat and burning sun, instead creating shadows and breezes, bringing plants and birds into their homes, and embracing a nature they had made kinder.

Left: The façade of Bayt al-Suhaymi along Harat al-Darb al-Asfar, a street one block north of the Mosque of al-Aqmar, gives no idea of the bright and airy world within.

Above: Entering from the street, your first view of Bayt al-Suhaymi is across the garden courtyard. You will want to wander, to enjoy the perspectives across the court from every possible angle and elevation. In fact it is two houses knocked together, one built in 1648, the other in 1796, and which continued to be privately inhabited until 1961.

Right and far right: Looking back across the central courtyard from within the shady recesses of the house.

Top left: The view into the courtyard from an upper room through the open shutter of a *mashrabiya* screen.

Left: Looking down into the courtyard garden from an open loggia above the entrance. In rooms like this you can sit down and rest and let the ambience of the place seduce you.

Above and right: Filtered light seeps into rooms through *mashrabiya* screens and stained glass windows. Wandering through the house you discover women's bedrooms, their windows tightly latticed, or the harem reception room overlooking the garden, its floors of marble and its walls covered with the most delicate green and blue plant-patterned tiles. Throughout the house there are many cupboards with carved and painted decorations.

Far right: Bayt al-Suhaymi seen from across a second court at the rear.

Above and left: The massive brooding minarets of the Mosque of al-Hakim are buttressed by great trapezoidal bases; the Mamluks added the pepper pot domes in which incense was burned, the scent drifting over the city.

Right: Looking into the city through Bab al-Nasr, built with Bab al-Futuh in 1087 by the same Armenian who built Bab Zuwayla.

Far right: One of the great bastion-like minarets of al-Hakim's mosque rises between Bab al-Futuh, in the foreground, and Bab al-Nasr. These gates, covered galleries, and crenelated bulwarks along the northern walls of the Fatimid city are masterpieces of medieval military architecture.

The Mosque of al-Hakim and the Northern Gates

Where Muizz Street approaches the northern walls of the medieval city, it runs along the flank of the **Mosque of al-Hakim**, completed in 1010. The place long had a baleful aura and was avoided for worship; as recently as 1980 the mosque was ruinous. But now that it has been restored, perhaps over-restored, the bright glitter of white marble and gold leaf have largely erased the dark legacy of al-Hakim, the third Fatimid caliph to rule from Cairo.

From the start of his reign al-Hakim was highly capricious; suddenly in 1004 he began his persecutions. Christians were forced to walk around carrying heavy crosses, and Jews had to wear clogs around their necks. Over the next ten years al-Hakim destroyed thirty thousand churches in Egypt and the Middle East, including the Church of the Holy Sepulcher in Jerusalem. Then in 1016 al-Hakim had himself proclaimed God at Friday prayers in Cairo. When Muslims protested, he burnt down half of Cairo and carried out summary decapitations, in the company, he said, of Adam and Solomon who hovered about him disguised as angels. Al-Hakim disappeared in 1021 while in the Moqattam Hills overlooking Cairo where he liked to look for portents in the stars; probably he was killed by his sister Setalmulq, whom he had intended to marry.

Beside the mosque is **Bab al-Futuh**, the Gate of Conquests, through which the great caravan of pilgrims passed each year on its way to Mecca, after making its way along Muizz Street, Darb al-Ahmar, and Bab al-Wazir Street from the Citadel. The gate is similar to Bab Zuwayla, with projecting oval towers, though the masonry is finer and the impression greater, for the space outside it has been cleared and there is a magnificent view of the ensemble of Bab al-Futuh, **Bab al-Nasr** (the Gate of Victory, to the east), the linking **Fatimid wall**, and al-Hakim's minarets.

The City of the Dead

The **Eastern Cemetery** or City of the Dead lies to the east of the medieval city. It is the burial ground of the Mamluk sultans and others of rank or fame right up to the present day. But the humble are buried here too, and the poor have always made their homes here, as have the keepers of family tombs. As many as half a million people are thought to be living in the City of the Dead and, with shops and stalls giving it the appearance of a residential suburb, it is hard to say where the tombs end and the city of the living begins.

The mausoleums of the Mamluk sultans Barquq, Ashraf Baybars, and Qaytbay, listing them from north to south, are the most outstanding buildings in the Eastern Cemetery.

The **Mausoleum of Barquq**, completed in 1411, has an open court surrounded by arcades. At either end of the eastern arcade with its prayer niches facing Mecca are large domed tomb chambers for Sultan Barquq and his family. This is the same Barquq who had

Above: A general view of the City of the Dead with the Moqattam Hills behind as seen from al-Azhar Park. The large *iwan* at the center belongs to the mausoleum of Umm Anuk, the favorite wife of Sultan al-Nasr.

Right: The City of the Dead is also home to the living.

Left, top and bottom: The Mausoleum of Barquq, its tomb interior and dome decoration. These were the first stone domes in Cairo; the zigzag ribbing was to develop into the elaborate polygons of the dome atop Qaytbay's mausoleum.

already built a mausoleum next to those of Qalaun and al-Nasr in Muizz Street; he was a formidable fighter against the Mongols and the Ottomans, but overcome by piety in his older years he wished to be buried near some holy sheikhs in the Eastern Cemetery.

Following the paved but dusty road south you come to the **Mausoleum of Sultan Ashraf Baybars** (also known as Barsbay) who captured Cyprus from the Christians. Built in 1432, its appeal is in its few but delicately worked elaborations, in particular the exterior of the dome, which in place of simple ribs or chevrons was the first to bear polygonal decorations.

Farther south is the **Mausoleum of Qaytbay**, completed in 1474 and a jewel of Mamluk architecture, comparable to the mosques of Ibn Tulun and Sultan Hasan. Unlike them it is free with decoration, but like them uses its decoration to great effect, as on its dome where the frequent play of filigree flowers upon star-shaped polygons has been described as "a song for two voices," a geometrical base with floral melody. The splendor of Qaytbay's reign marked the apogee of Mamluk vigor; two decades later Cairo fell to the Ottomans.

Top left: The Mausoleum of Qaytbay. Along with al-Nasr, Qaytbay was the grandest of the Mamluk builders, constructing both religious and secular buildings throughout the Middle East, as well as in Cairo and in Alexandria where the fort that bears his name stands on the site of the ancient Pharos.

Above: If you climb up to the roof of Qaytbay's mausoleum you can see at closer hand the tracery of stone carving on the dome and minaret, which is as delicate as previous periods had managed in wood and stucco.

Bottom far left: The great portal, in red and white *ablaq*, a decorative masonry technique of alternating stones, leading into Qaytbay's mausoleum.

Bottom left: The immense height of the tomb chamber draws the walls into the ascending dome. The decoration of ceilings, pavings, arches, and windows inside the Mausoleum of Qaytbay is breathtakingly variegated, yet overall it is measured and subdued.

Right: A man reads the Quran while sitting against the *minbar* in the Mausoleum of Baybars.

Downtown Cairo

A thousand years ago, when the Fatimids founded al-Qahira, the bed of the Nile was far more to the east than now. From the fortress of Babylon in Old Cairo it cut a diagonal course toward the northeast so that it flowed no more than a kilometer to the west of al-Azhar, not the three kilometers of today. Where we see the streets of downtown Cairo there was only water.

New land became available as the Nile shifted westward, but it was left unoccupied until Muhammad Ali brought new prosperity to Egypt after centuries of decline and blight under the Ottoman occupation. In 1845 Muhammad Ali drew up plans for a broadened and extended Musky Street which runs east to Khan al-Khalili, and for the construction of al-Qalaa Street which heads southeast out to the Citadel—the roads converging to the west at what would become Midan Ataba, which now lies between downtown Cairo and the medieval city.

But it was the Khedive Ismail, Muhammad Ali's grandson, who set in motion the plan for the **westernized Cairo** that became the downtown of today. Ismail visited Paris in 1867 where he was greatly impressed with the marvelous city of broad boulevards, formal gardens, grand department stores, and covered shopping arcades that had been built for Napoleon III by Baron Haussmann, his prefect of the Seine.

Ismail wanted to do for Cairo what Haussmann had done for Paris, but unlike Haussmann, who had pulled down much of the old quarters of the city, Ismail could extend westward on land reclaimed from the Nile. The khedive gave the task to Ali Mubarak, his minister of public works, who had been born of humble origins in a Delta village but was sent on one of Muhammad Ali's educational missions to France where he studied military and civil engineering.

Within two years, in time for the celebrations to mark the

Above: Midan Talaat Harb, named for the financier Muhammad Talaat Harb, founder of Bank Misr, the first Egyptian bank, in 1920. Behind are the Baehler Buildings, built by the Swiss Charles Baehler, a miniature version of the Rue de Rivoli in Paris.

Right: Built by a Swiss chocolatier in 1925 and adorned with art deco mosaics, Groppi in Midan Talaat Harb is Cairo's most famous tea room.

Far and center left: The Muhammad Shawarbi Pasha Building, at the corner of Ramesses and 26th of July Streets, dates from 1925.

Left: The Grand Hotel in Midan Orabi is a 1930s art deco survival.

opening of the Suez Canal in 1869, Mubarak had built the core of the modern city round **Ezbekiya**, a filled-in lake which itself was turned into gardens laid out by the Frenchman who had done the Bois de Boulogne in Paris. An opera house, modeled on La Scala, was built by an Italian near by. A new street, Clot Bey Street, linked the train station to the north with Midan Ataba, adjacent to Ezbekiya. **Midan Ataba** soon became Cairo's transportation hub and a main commercial center, containing the city's central post office and its principal fire station, as it still does, as well as department stores, the central food market, and some elegant hotels.

The plan also positioned a number of squares to the west between Ezbekiya and the Nile, among them **midans Mustafa Kamel, Orabi, Talaat Harb, Lazughli, and al-Tahrir**, to give them their current names, and it traced out their radiating avenues which form Cairo's interlocking street pattern of today. This new city was known for some time as Ismailia, after the khedive. Spaces were filled in by Parisian-style commercial and residential buildings, the new city's cosmopolitan residents and visitors were served by French and English bookshops, tea rooms and pavement cafés, smart shops,

Below: Near the Ezbekiya Gardens, this equestrian statue of Ibrahim Pasha, son of Muhammad Ali, stands in front of the multi-story car park that has replaced the Opera House built in 1869. Khedive Ismail commissioned Verdi to write *Aida* to celebrate the opening of the Suez Canal. In the event, *Aida* was late and *Rigoletto* was performed instead before a glittering international audience which included the Empress Eugénie, wife of Napoleon III.

The base of Ibrahim's statue records his victories, which were considerable; by 1833 his armies had conquered the whole of the Middle East and stood within a few days' march of Constantinople, giving his father the chance to overthrow the Ottoman Empire, which Muhammad Ali recoiled from doing. Ibrahim began his military career in 1818 when he drove the Wahhabis out of Mecca and Medina where they were imposing their fundamentalist version of Islam, and sent their leader Abdullah ibn Saud to Constantinople where the Ottoman sultan struck off his head. A hundred or so years later and the Wahhabis, still under the leadership of the Saud family, made themselves rulers of what they now call Saudi Arabia.

Left: A statue of the early twentieth-century nationalist Mustafa Kamel stands in the square that bears his name and looks along Emad al-Din Street.

Right: El Haty, off 26th of July Street near the Windsor Hotel, is one of the older restaurants of Cairo, renowned especially for its lamb dishes, which were a favorite of King Farouk's. Inside, the place sparkles when they bother to turn on the lights; mirrors cover the walls and brilliant chandeliers hang from the high ceiling.

Below: In the 1920s the Windsor Hotel was ranked by Baedeker as just below the old Shepheard's round the corner near Ezbekiya Gardens, since when it has not changed a jot: the character is literally peeling off its walls. It has a delightful bar-cum-dining room-cum-lounge hung with weird curios and damaged paintings, where beers are served by robed and long-dead waiters.

Bottom right: Built in 1905 in neo-pharaonic style, the Shaar Hashamaim (Gates of Heaven) Synagogue in Adly Street still serves what remains of Cairo's Sephardic Jewish community. Tablets inside record the names of major benefactor families, among them Mosseri, Suares, Cattaoui, Rolo, Ades, Harari, Naggar, Cicurel, and Curiel, who accounted for much of Egypt's banks, department stores, transport companies, and urban development projects.

and grand department stores modeled on the finest in Paris, and no less grand hotels, while cinemas and skating rinks were added later. Ismail's dream of building a new Paris on the Nile was rapidly coming true, and soon Cairo was internationally recognized as a delightful metropolis whose amenities surpassed those of many European and American cities.

By the end of the nineteenth century there were two Cairos, contiguous but continents apart culturally and centuries apart technologically. To the east lay the native city, still essentially pre-industrial in technology, social structure, and way of life; to the west lay the cosmopolitan city of Greeks, Italians, Armenians, British, French, Swiss, Jews, Syro-Lebanese, and others, its faster pace and European identity an expression of the new industrial age. To the east lay a labyrinth of unpaved streets, its closely packed neighborhoods unrelieved by trees or green spaces; to the west lay broad straight paved streets flanked by wide pavements and adorned with flower beds and French-style formal gardens. You entered the eastern city by caravan and traversed it on foot, for its lanes were too narrow for wheeled traffic; the western city was entered by railway and traversed by carriage.

Italians played a prominent role in Cairo, whether as laborers, contractors, or architects. Drawing on the Italian renaissance, they gave their buildings a Tuscan cast, while others used an Italian Gothic reminiscent of Venice. French baroque, with its delicate ironwork balconies and ornate cantilevers, its marble steps and entrances, and its molded architraves, also appeared throughout downtown. By the 1920s both European and Egyptian architects had adopted art deco into which they frequently incorporated an eclectic mix of Islamic and pharaonic motifs.

Over the last half century or so, unchecked population growth, calamitous economic policies, flawed planning regulations, and a lack of civic responsibility have all had their deleterious effect on downtown Cairo, but something of what was handsome still remains.

Bottom left: View from the Cairo Tower on Gezira toward downtown Cairo with the Moqattam Hills in the distance. Qasr al-Aini Bridge in the foreground leads to Midan al-Tahrir, which with its numerous international luxury hotels as well as the Egyptian Museum, is the modern heart of tourist Cairo. Midan al-Tahrir, which means Liberation Square, had its name changed by Nasser from the original Midan Ismailia, built on a drained swamp by Khedive Ismail. The bridge, likewise named after Ismail, was the first modern bridge to cross the Nile at Cairo.

Below: An impromptu pavement café on al-Gumhuriya Street where the old houses have been turned into workshops. The original and famous old Shepheard's Hotel, whose guest list included General Gordon and Sir Richard Burton, and where everyone who was anyone was seen on the terrace drinking four o'clock tea, stood on the corner of al-Gumhuriya and Alfi Streets at the northwest corner of Ezbekiya Gardens. It was burnt down by rioters in 1952.

Right: The mausoleum erected for Saad Zaghloul, the early twentieth-century nationalist leader and prime minister of Egypt, near the intersection of Saad Zaghloul and Mansour Streets. "The present movement in Egypt," said Zaghloul in 1919, "is not a religious movement, for Muslims and Copts demonstrate together, and neither is it a xenophobic movement or a movement calling for Arab unity." Zaghloul envisioned a secular and progressive Egypt along European lines. When the British deported Zaghloul to Malta in March 1919, the whole of Egypt rose in revolt, not only against the British, but against traditional constraints, so that it was now that Muslim women first tore off their veils.

Bottom left: The grandiose atrium of the Sednoui department store is just north of Midan Ataba. Founded in 1913 by the Christian Syrian Sednoui brothers in emulation of Galleries Lafayette on Boulevard Haussmann in Paris, the store was considered second only to the Jewish-owned Cicurel on Fuad Street (now 26th of July Street) in setting the trends of Cairo consumer fashion. In 1961 Sednoui, along with Egypt's other major department stores, was nationalized, since when it has become a complete stranger to enterprise. But as a monument it is one of the grandest in all Cairo.

Bottom right: Tiring department store on Midan Ataba, its glass cupola resting on the shoulders of four Herculean statues, was once the luxurious purveyor of Paris perfumes and haute couture, English cloth, and German housewares, but is now the home of hundreds of squatters and sweatshops. In 1913 when Victor Tiring, an Austro-Hungarian lately from Constantinople, opened his store in Midan Ataba, the square commanded two worlds, to the east the bustling market district along Musky Street and stretching away to Khan al-Khalili, and to the west Ezbekiya Gardens and the smart boulevards radiating through the European quarters of Ismailia. But soon it was outclassed by rival department stores located in the heart of downtown, and already in the 1930s had been invaded by seedy shops, offices, and warehouses. Today it rises above a lively street market which rages day and evening.

Garden City

Immediately south of the British and American embassies between Qasr al-Aini and the Nile lies the fashionable residential and diplomatic quarter called **Garden City**. Developed before the First World War and inspired by garden suburb communities then growing up in Britain, the area is a latticework of winding tree-shaded streets with a rural atmosphere in contrast to the geometrical regularity of downtown Cairo, which was laid out in formal French style.

The entire area was reclaimed during Muhammad Ali's reign when its swamps and sandy mounds became the grounds of riverside palaces for Ibrahim Pasha and Khedive Ismail's mother. The palaces are recalled in many of the names of Garden City's streets, such as Saray al-Qobba, grand palace; Harass, guards; Diwan, ministry; not to mention various attendant facilities such as Tolombat, pumps; Warshet al-Tambak, gilded pewter factory; and Dar al-Shifa, house of recovery.

Laid out in a dreamlike pattern of intersecting rounded rectangles and triangles, it is easy to lose all sense of direction, and not infrequently you end up where you had begun. Nor is it any help that while walking down a street, you find that its name has changed and then in some vague and unannounced way has changed and changed again.

All of which lends a charm to Garden City, where it is enjoyable to wander round aimlessly observing the architectural variety, where no two buildings are alike, and delicacy and invention are found in every detail.

Above: Built in 1908 by a German financier in Italian Renaissance style, the Bayerlé Palace on Nabatat and Ahmad Pasha Streets was subsequently a girls' school, then the home of Chahine Serageddin, a landed pasha and his large family, but since his son's death in 2000 it has stood deserted and overgrown.

Top right: A leafy curving street in Garden City.

Center right: The British Embassy, at the northern end of Garden City, was built in 1893. Until 1954, before the construction of the Corniche, its grounds came right down to the Nile. Between 1882, when Britain occupied Egypt, until independence in 1936, the occupant of this building, though he bore the humble title of Agent or later High Commissioner, was the de facto ruler of Egypt. There remains a closeness, on more equal terms, in the relations between the two countries, with Britain the largest non-Arab investor in Egypt.

Bottom left: Though shuttered and gray with dust there is elegance still in the design of this stained glass window and its ornately decorated cornice.

Bottom right: Art deco gate and bow window.

Left: During the Second World War Egypt was vital to Britain's hopes of success against the German–Italian Axis which had overrun the whole of Europe. Had Egypt fallen to Rommel, then the entire Middle East, Turkey and Iran, and the Mediterranean too, would have fallen to fascist rule. Cairo was therefore second only to London as a center for British war operations, and between 1940 and 1945 Garden City was virtually taken over by the British for use as offices and residences. Ten Tolombat Street was famous during the war when it was known as Gray Pillars or simply 'Number 10'—a reference to 10 Downing Street in London. From 1941 it became the headquarters of the minister of state for the Middle East. Appointed by the War Cabinet in London, his function was to regulate the often conflicting priorities of the various British ambassadors and military commanders in the region. Oliver Lyttelton was the first to hold the position, followed by the Australian Richard Casey, then by the Anglo-Irishman Walter Edward Guinness, Lord Moyne, who was murdered in Cairo in 1944 by the Stern Gang, a Jewish terrorist group, which saw the British presence in the Middle East as the chief obstacle to the realization of a Jewish state.

Above: Prince Muhammad Ali's residential palace half-hidden in the lush garden of semi-tropical trees.

Left: The ground-floor entrance foyer in the residential palace, its eclectic collection including wall tiles, painted glass, oriental carpets, colossal Turkish chandeliers, and architectural elements salvaged from crumbling Mamluk and Ottoman buildings.

Below: An Ottoman-style reception room in the prince's residence.

Manyal Palace

As recently as the 1940s Roda Island, which lies along the east bank of the Nile between Garden City and Old Cairo, remained incongruously rural, with flocks of goats and sheep wandering amid fields and villages, though they were being fast displaced by rising blocks of flats. In 1900 when Prince Muhammad Ali Tawfiq built his palace overlooking a narrow branch of the river, the island was entirely bucolic. Today, in accordance with the prince's wishes, **Manyal Palace** is open to the public (entrance on al-Saray Street, open 9am–4:30pm daily; admission charge), an oasis of opulence and greenery from another time.

Prince Muhammad Ali, who was a grandson of Khedive Ismail and the uncle of King Farouk, envisioned Manyal, which is in fact several palaces distributed about the grounds in the Turkish manner, as a showpiece for Islamic art. He drew on the Fatimid, Mamluk, and Ottoman styles familiar to Cairo but also applied Persian, Syrian, Moroccan, and Andalusian embellishments to his buildings, which include the reception palace in the main gate, the residential palace sequestered among banyans, and a pavilion containing a reproduction of Muhammad Ali Pasha's throne room atop the Citadel. Elsewhere in the gardens, which are filled with cedar, royal palm, and Indian rubber trees, the prince built a private mosque, but he was not responsible for the grotesque hunting hall added in Nasser's time to display King Farouk's trophies, among them a table made of elephants' ears and a stuffed hermaphrodite goat.

Gezira

Sometime around 1300 **Gezira** emerged from the Nile as a shifting sandbank. The name itself means 'island,' but over the centuries it has sometimes been three islands, or has joined itself to the western bank of the river and not been an island at all. Gezira was stabilized only during the reign of Khedive Ismail who dug a channel to divide it permanently from the far shoreline and raised the island to protect it from the Nile's annual flood.

Within a few years Gezira became both fashionable and easy to reach. Ismail built a palace here to accommodate the Empress Eugenie, wife of Napoleon III, during her visit for the opening of the Suez Canal in 1869, its extensive gardens landscaped by the same Frenchman who laid out the gardens at Ezbekiya. Three years later Ismail commissioned French civil engineers to construct Gezira Bridge toward the southern end of the island, the first bridge across the Nile. But under the khedive's rule Egypt's borrowings got out of

Left: Gezira seen from atop the Hyatt hotel on Roda Island to the south. Three kilometers long by a kilometer wide, Gezira enjoys vast expanses of green, a legacy of the grounds and gardens once surrounding the palace built by Khedive Ismail in 1869. The island has been stable only since the 1860s, when it was raised clear of the annual Nile floods, themselves controlled since 1902 with the construction of the low dam at Aswan in Upper Egypt. Three bridges can be seen along the main channel of the Nile: nearest is Qasr al-Aini Bridge built in 1933 which replaced the original 1872 bridge, the first across the Nile; in the distance is 26th of July Bridge built in 1912. Between the two is the Sixth October Bridge, which is not so much a means of reaching Gezira as a direct link from downtown to the west bank of the Nile. Called the spinal cord of Cairo, the Sixth of October of Bridge is in fact a vast series of interlinking roadways and flyovers which took thirty years to build, from 1969 to 1999. The Qasr al-Aini Bridge directly connects Midan al-Tahrir in downtown Cairo with the Cairo Tower, the Opera House, and the Museum of Egyptian Modern Art on Gezira.

Bottom left: A pair of magnificent lions guards each end of the Qasr al-Aini Bridge. They are the work of the French sculptor Alfred Henri Jacquemart and were originally intended to surround the base of the equestrian statue of Muhammad Ali in Alexandria, but the builders of the 1872 bridge thought they would do better service here, as they continue to do at either end of the 1933 bridge.

Bottom right: Modern sculpture by Ahmed El-Setouhi outside the Museum of Egyptian Modern Art which, along with the new Opera House, is near where the Qasr al-Aini Bridge crosses from downtown to Gezira.

Top: Looking across to Gezira from the Hyatt Hotel on the east bank of the Nile. The tall tower at the southern tip of Gezira is the al-Gezira Sheraton. To its right you can see the low dome of the Opera House and also the Cairo Tower.

Below left: Girl with a Headscarf, a 1943 painting by Mahmoud Said in the Museum of Egyptian Modern Art. Admission charge.

Below right: Statue of the nationalist leader Saad Zaghloul by Mahmoud Mokhtar. It was raised on Gezira in 1938 at the same moment as another statue of Zaghloul by Mokhtar was raised in Alexandria.

Bottom left and right: Using Arab motifs, the new Opera House was built with Japanese assistance in 1989.

control, and after his deposition in 1879 his palace on Gezira was sold off by his creditors and became a hotel, then for a generation became home to the wealthy Syrian Lotfallah family. The palace grounds, which contained a race course and polo field, became the elite **Gezira Sporting Club**, while to the west of the palace was Ismail's fish grotto, eventually opened to the public as an aquarium and park in 1902.

In 1912 a second bridge and cross-island thoroughfare, both now known as 26th of July, were built. They separated the once royal enclosure from the still marshy farmland at the northern tip of the island. But already by 1907 a Swiss property developer, Charles Baehler, who later built the handsome Baehler Buildings downtown in Midan Talaat Harb, purchased all of northern Gezira from a missionary society and subdivided it into lots. Named **Zamalek**, a name of uncertain meaning, but possibly from the Albanian for straw hut, it was less fashionable than the area to the south, often called

Above: The racetrack at the Gezira Sporting Club. The club occupies nearly a third of the entire island.

Left: The Cairo Tower rises 187 meters and offers marvelous panoramas from its enclosed and revolving fourteenth- and fifteenth-level dining areas and its open sixteenth-level observation platform (open 9am–1am; admission charge).

Top right: The Fish Garden is a popular meeting place for young lovers.

Center right: The shady gardens overlooking the narrow channel of the Nile at Gezira are also a favorite with couples.

Bottom right: Fishermen ply their boats in the shallows off Gezira.

Gezira Gardens. But now all the developed area on Gezira is called Zamalek, and like Garden City, if not more so, its leafy streets are the favored addresses for diplomats, resident foreigners, and wealthy Egyptians, making it the most cosmopolitan part of Cairo.

Today nothing remains of Ismail's palace except the salamlek, or reception quarters, which forms the core of the Marriott Hotel. The 1872 Gezira Bridge was replaced in 1933 by the present Qasr al-Aini Bridge, built at the same time and by the same British firm as the Sydney Harbor Bridge. But Ismail has left his legacy all the same in the green and open spaces of the island which bring pleasure to Cairenes to this day. Not least, at the southern end of the former palace grounds, is the cultural park which contains the handsome new **Opera House** and the **Museum of Egyptian Modern Art**. Nearby rises the **Cairo Tower**, inaugurated in 1961, which has come to symbolize the city itself.

Top left: The Islamic Ceramics Museum on al-Gezira Street in Zamalek contains works from all periods from the Fatimid to the Ottoman; entrance is free.

Top right: The Episcopal Cathedral of All Saints in Zamalek has been designed in the shape of a lotus.

Bottom left: This art deco building at 14 Salih Ayyub Street in Zamalek was home to the novelist Lawrence Durrell in 1941 before he was transferred to Alexandria where he began drafting *The Alexandria Quartet.*

Bottom center and right: Blocks of art deco flats overlooking the Nile along Saray al-Gezira Street in Zamalek.

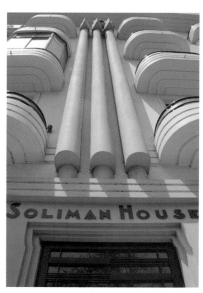

Right: View from a penthouse flat in Zamalek looking toward new skyscrapers built on the east bank of the Nile.

Bottom left: The Helwan University Faculty of Music in Zamalek's Shagarat al-Durr Street was originally a private villa built by Italian architects in Venetian Gothic style.

Bottom center: Now the Greater Cairo Library on Muhammad Mazhar Street in Zamalek, this was originally the home of Musa Yaqub Cattaoui, head of one of Egypt's wealthiest Jewish families.

Bottom right: A visit to the Greater Cairo Library is an opportunity to look around inside one of Zamalek's finest villas, which was well preserved and restored when it was converted to public use.

The Egyptian Museum

Built in 1902 on a riverside site that was then one of the quietest areas of Cairo, the venerable **Egyptian Museum** (open 9am–4:45pm daily; admission charge) now finds itself on the north side of Midan al-Tahrir, the city's busiest traffic intersection, where it suffers from vibration and pollution. A new state-of-the-art museum is being built out by the Pyramids which will house the complete Tutankhamun collection and other more vulnerable objects. The older museum will be refurbished and will display monumental stone statues and other large objects of the Old and New Kingdoms. But all that is some years away.

The museum contains 120,000 catalogued objects, of which 44,000 are on display at any one time. Allowing one minute for each exhibit on display, you could see everything in about four months. The average guided tour lasts two hours. The collection is arranged more or less chronologically, so that starting at the entrance and walking clockwise round the ground floor you pass from Old

Top left and right: Some ancient statues and reliefs are exhibited in the gardens of the Egyptian Museum. Its façade is adorned with two female figures representing Upper and Lower Egypt.

Bottom left: The exhibits in the museum cover the entirety of antiquity in Egypt, from predynastic to Roman times. This very fine Old Kingdom diorite statue is of the Fourth Dynasty pharaoh Chephren. The falcon god Horus embraces Chephren's head with his wings, granting him divine authority and protection. Chephren built the second of the great Pyramids at Giza, and he also ordered a rocky outcrop in the area of his funerary complex to be carved into the Sphinx.

Bottom right: Some of the most affecting exhibits in the museum are the encaustic portraits (colors mixed into molten wax) of Greeks and Romans living in the Fayyum. They adopted the Egyptian practice of embalming and had these portraits done to bind onto their mummies at death. The technique is superb, with shading, highlighting, and perspective; they are living faces in which you can read whole lives.

Right: A granite statue of the lion-headed goddess Sekhmet dating from the New Kingdom. She had two aspects to her personality, one dangerous and destructive, the other healing and protective.

Kingdom to Middle and New Kingdom exhibits, concluding with Ptolemaic and Roman exhibits. The upper floor contains prehistoric and early dynastic exhibits and the contents of several tombs, including Tutankhamun's. His gold mask and two of his three golden sarcophaguses are on display in the museum along with 1,700 other magnificently crafted items that were buried with him and which altogether take up two entire galleries.

The mummy room is also on the upper floor. Here some of the mightiest figures in ancient Egyptian history lie shriveled and half-naked in glass cases. Among them are the New Kingdom pharaohs Seti I, serene and majestic, and his son Ramesses II, who looks as though he is straining to awaken: as his mummy was unwrapped, his arms rose from his chest, his hands opened and his fingers uncurled. With them is Ramesses' son Merneptah whom some say was the pharaoh of the Exodus. Tutankhamun's mummy remains in his tomb at Luxor.

The basement of the museum presents special exhibitions; the entrance is round the left-hand side, and a separate entry fee is payable.

Top left: Akhenaten was the New Kingdom heretic pharaoh who overthrew Egypt's polytheistic religion in favor of the worship of a single god, the Aten, which was represented in the form of the sun's disc. His revolution did not last, and during the reign of his son Tutankhamun the worship of many gods under the supremacy of Amun-Ra was restored. About a third of the entire museum is taken up with exhibits from the New Kingdom's Eighteenth Dynasty, particularly with Tutankhamun and his immediate ancestors, his father Akhenaten, his grandparents Amenophis III and Queen Tiy, and his great grandparents Yuya and Tuyu.

Top right: Akhenaten's chief wife was the exquisitely elegant Nefertiti, but it was a secondary wife who gave birth to Tutankhamun.

Bottom left: The style of art during Akhenaten's reign was vividly naturalistic, as in this fragment of paving from his royal palace.

Below: This funerary bed decorated with hippopotamus heads is one of the 1,700 objects from the tomb of Tutankhamun that are on display in the museum.

Right: Tutankhamun's mummy was placed inside three golden coffins which in turn were placed inside four gilded shrines, as gold was believed to protect the body from corruption. Likewise his internal organs were separately mummified and enclosed within a gilded shrine, and this was protected by four gilded goddesses, Nephthys, Isis, Selkis, and Neith, who is shown here.

Bottom left: Tutankhamun's gold mask shows the features of a young man. He was probably no more than nineteen when he died.

Bottom right: Tutankhamun's tomb was stuffed with items he would need for the afterlife, among them this golden throne. Its sumptuously inlaid back panel shows Tutankhamun with his wife Ankhesenamun within a pavilion decked with flowers and beneath the life-giving rays of the sun. Ankhesenamun was the daughter of Nefertiti by Akhenaten and therefore Tutankhamun's half-sister.

Memphis and Saqqara

Memphis, the first capital of a united Egypt, stood on the west bank of the Nile about twenty kilometers south of Cairo, its modern-day successor. Founded around 3000 B.C. and surrounded by high white walls, the fortress-city controlled the land and water routes between Upper and Lower Egypt. Built for the span of the living, its mud-brick palaces and shrines have now vanished; but **Saqqara**, the necropolis of Memphis on the desert plateau six kilometers to the west, was built of stone to endure eternity and survives to this day. (Both sites are open 8am–4pm daily in winter, and 8am–4pm daily in summer; admission charge.)

About 300 years after unification, that is around 2686 B.C., Egypt entered a long period of security and order known to us as the Old Kingdom. During the reign of Zoser there was a sudden use and mastery of stone at Saqqara. His mortuary complex of courts and

Left: In replicating the walled mud-brick city of Memphis, Zoser created at Saqqara the world's first city of stone.

Right: The Step Pyramid built for Zoser marked the beginning of the new pyramidal form. Symbolically it was the means by which Zoser could ascend to the heavens, a star among eternal stars.

Bottom left: At the north face of the Step Pyramid there is the serdab, a masonry box, tilted slightly back and with two small holes drilled through its front panel. Looking in, you see a life-size limestone statue of Zoser, like a strapped-in astronaut in his space capsule, his eyes fixed through the holes on the North Star, awaiting blast-off and immortality. The circumpolar stars and the North Star itself were "those that know no destruction," for they never set and so never died; this was the place of eternal blessedness for which Egyptians longed. If Zoser's *ka* still inhabits this statue, then perhaps in the dark of night it rockets starward and mingles with the universe.

Below: These delicate and beautifully proportioned engaged columns on a sanctuary façade have the form of a papyrus plant, the shaft the triangular stem, the capital the fanning head. Zoser's funerary complex is full of imitative references to rush matting, reed, and wood forms.

Below: Today the centuries of Nile silt have swallowed Memphis entirely, so much so that it is impossible to soliloquize on how the mighty has fallen—there is, simply, so little to stir reflection.

chapels, 544 meters long and 277 meters wide, surrounded by a wall ten meters high, reproduced in beautifully detailed and architectured stone the mud-brick city of Memphis. And dominating Zoser's sacred enclosure at Saqqara was the first pyramid, over sixty-two meters high, built in steps.

In the symbolism of its form as a stairway to the stars and in the durability of its material the Step Pyramid was meant to ensure eternal life for Zoser's *ka*, that is his soul; likewise its surrounding mortuary complex was an eternal promise in stone that even in the afterlife Zoser would perform the necessary rituals by which Egypt would enjoy continued order and perpetual regeneration. Here a replica was built of the field of the Heb Sed or jubilee race that would have taken place at Memphis, when a king renewed his claim to the throne by running between two markers representing Upper and Lower Egypt, thereby demonstrating his continued vitality that in turn he conferred upon the land. Next to this was the Heb Sed court flanked by chapels, one for the priesthood of each province who, receiving jubilee gifts from the king, would return home under an obligation to recognize his supremacy over their local deities and to put their service at his ultimate disposal. The original of these chapels at Memphis would have been tent-like structures supported by poles, cross-supports, and other fixtures of wood, reed, papyrus, and the like; at Saqqara these were mimicked in carved columns, capitals, cornices, and moldings, so inventing the language of architecture in stone.

The Pyramids

The eleven-kilometer-long road from central Cairo once passed across fields which would flood with the rising of the Nile, but nowadays the entire route has been built up until it reaches the Mena House Hotel. There the road curves sharply to the left and mounts a gentle slope to the **Pyramids of Giza** which stand, as they have done for 4,600 years, on the edge of the desert plateau (open 8am–4pm daily in winter, 8am–5pm daily in summer; admission charge). The nearest is the Great Pyramid, containing the tomb of Cheops, the Fourth Dynasty pharaoh who ruled Egypt during the Old Kingdom. This is the oldest and largest of the group; it was built in about 2570 B.C. and the others, built by his son Chephren and his grandson Mycerinus, stand in descending order of age and size along a southwest axis; when built they were probably aligned precisely with the North Star, their entrance corridors aiming straight at it.

Above: The pyramids (from left to right) of Mycerinus, Chephren, and Cheops stand on the edge of the desert plateau overlooking Cairo. They are accompanied by lesser pyramids for royal wives.

Top left: Seen across the gardens of the Mena House Hotel, the Great Pyramid of Cheops is, in terms of volume, the largest monument on earth.

Bottom left: Chephren, the son of Cheops, had a rocky outcrop carved into the Sphinx. The largest statue of the ancient world, its body is the protective lion of sacred places and its face most likely represents Chephren as the sun god.

Right: In 1215 the Ayyubid Sultan al-Adil decided to sell off the stones from the Pyramids to building contractors. His workmen began with the Pyramid of Mycerinus, but they found it more difficult to dismantle than it had been for the ancient Egyptians to construct it, and after eight months they gave up.

Far right: You enter the Cheops Pyramid through an opening made by the ninth-century caliph al-Mamun. Coming from Baghdad to suppress an uprising of Copts in the Delta, he took the opportunity to search for treasure, but the pyramid had already been robbed after the collapse of the Old Kingdom.

At first the second pyramid, that of Chephren, seems largest, but that is because it stands on higher ground and retains its casing toward its peak. Its present height is 136.4 meters (originally 143 meters) and its volume is 2,200,000 cubic meters; this compares with a height of 137.2 meters (originally 146.6 meters) for the Great Pyramid of Cheops, which has a volume of 2,550,000 cubic meters.

Cheops' pyramid was built of over 2,500,000 enormous blocks of limestone cut from the Moqattam Hills and locally. Of these about 170,000, including the polished casing stones which once gave the Pyramids their perfectly smooth faces, were removed by Arabs and Turks and used in the construction of their monuments in Cairo.

Regarded by the Greeks as one of the seven wonders of the ancient world (and the only one to have survived more or less intact), the Pyramid of Cheops is the second most massive monument ever built by man (the pyramid at Cholula in Mexico, built nearly 4,000 years later and largely destroyed by the Spaniards, was 500,000 cubic meters greater in volume).

The Pyramid of Mycerinus is much smaller. It has a tenth of the volume of the other two and rises only to a height of 65.5 meters, but it is imposing all the same and contributes to the satisfying arrangement of the group.

Napoleon astonished his officers with the calculation that the stones from these three pyramids would be sufficient to build a wall three meters high and 0.3 meters thick around the whole of France.

Below: The best times to visit the pyramids are at dawn, at sunset, and at night when they form as much a part of the natural order as the sun, moon, and stars.

The star worship associated with the Step Pyramid at Saqqara coalesced with the sun worship expressed by the true pyramids with smoothly sloping sides at Giza. In Egyptian creation myths there is a primal hill which rises from the chaos of the waters. Until the twentieth century when a series of Nile dams and barrages finally put an end to the annual inundation, that was very much the scene in Egypt: villages huddled on mounds to avoid the flood; then when the waters subsided the sun drew the harvest from the silt. This primal hill, the *benben*, a word whose root, *bn*, is bound up with the notion of shining, brilliant, ascending, became associated with the cult of the sun-god Ra, who after the darkness of the night rose into the sky.

As the sun set every evening beneath the horizon of the Western Desert, the pyramids at Giza were a symbol and a promise that the reborn morning sun would bring life to all the land.